Fortress · 14

Fort
Wes

6

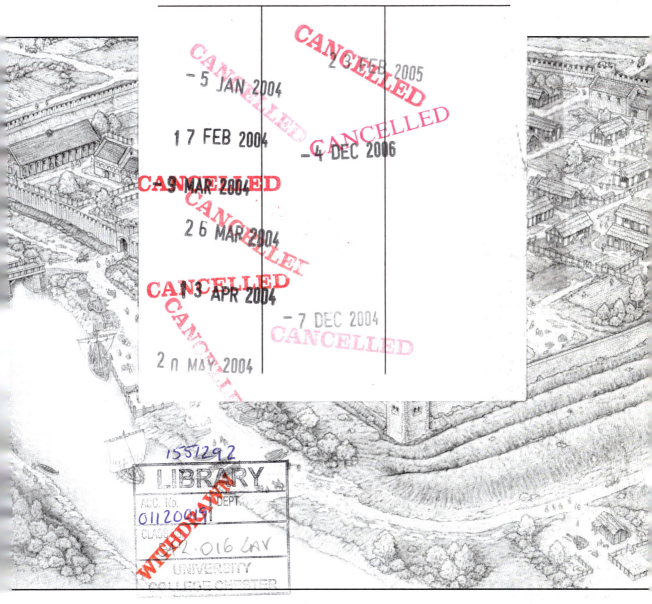

Ryan Lavelle · Illustrated by D Spedaliere & S S Spedaliere

Series editors Marcus Cowper and Nikolai Bogdanovic

First published in Great Britain in 2003 by Osprey Publishing, Elms Court,
Chapel Way, Botley, Oxford OX2 9LP, United Kingdom.
Email: info@ospreypublishing.com

ISBN 1 84176 639 9

Editorial by Ilios Publishing, Oxford, UK (www.iliospublishing.com)
Maps by The Map Studio, Romsey, UK
Index by Alison Worthington
Design: Ken Vail Graphic Design, Cambridge, UK
Originated by Grasmere Digital Imaging, Leeds, UK
Printed and bound by L-Rex Printing Company Ltd

03 04 05 06 07   10 9 8 7 6 5 4 3 2 1

A CIP catalogue record for this book is available from the British Library.

FOR A CATALOG OF ALL BOOKS PUBLISHED BY OSPREY MILITARY
AND AVIATION PLEASE CONTACT:

Osprey Direct USA, c/o MBI Publishing, P.O. Box 1,
729 Prospect Ave, Osceola, WI 54020, USA
E-mail: info@ospreydirectusa.com

Osprey Direct UK, P.O. Box 140, Wellingborough,
Northants, NN8 2FA, UK
E-mail: info@ospreydirect.co.uk

www.ospreypublishing.com

Artist's note

Our sincere thanks to all who have helped in the preparation of
this book. We would like to dedicate this book to our dearest
daughter Alina and to Lior and Rani, her wonderful cousins.
Readers may care to note that the original paintings from which
the color plates in this book were prepared are available for
private sale. All reproduction copyright whatsoever is retained by
the Publishers. All enquiries should be addressed to:

Sarah Sulemsohn
Tel-Fax: 00 39 0575 692210
info@alinaillustrazioni.com
alina@alinaillustrazioni.com
www.alinaillustrazioni.com

The Publishers regret that they can enter into no correspondence
upon this matter.

Dedication

For my parents, Don and Vee Lavelle.

Editor's note

Unless otherwise indicated, all illustrations apart from the colour
plates belong to the author.

Contents

Introduction

In an entry for the year 789, the *Anglo-Saxon Chronicle* recorded the first of what was to be a series of attacks on the kingdom of Wessex. A royal reeve, entrusted with ensuring the collection of tolls and taxes from traders, went down to the coast at Portland, Dorset, where three ships had drawn ashore and attempted to summon their crews to the king's manor. The visitors, from Hörthaland in Norway, were distinctly uncooperative and the reeve was promptly killed.

It was an inauspicious start for a terrifying movement that was to sweep across Western Europe in the following century, but it was perhaps fitting that this early attack should have been so implicitly concerned with trade. Attacks upon monasteries and churches, such as the better-known assault upon the monastery of Lindisfarne in 793, attracted the attention of the literate churchmen who dominated the recording of history. However, it was to be the economic as much as the religious impact of the Viking raids, which meant that the rulers of western Europe had to consider how they could best defend their realms against an increasingly dangerous external threat.

Wide-scale archaeological excavations of urban sites have shown that during the 8th century large 'international' trading sites had been placed under a high degree of royal control, with close attention paid to their layouts. Examples such as *Hamwic* (Southampton) and *Gippeswic* (Ipswich) in the Anglo-Saxon kingdoms and Quentovic and Dorestadt in the Frankish realms (now France and the Netherlands), show that kings had vested interests in controlling and promoting trade within their realms. Coins were minted in such places and royal manors were close by. The problem was that the only real protection for these sites was a recognition of the authority of the king as a giver of peace; beyond small ditches marking out the sites, there were no physical defences to speak of. These sites were obviously vulnerable to an increasingly dangerous threat.

By the early-9th century, Anglo-Saxon England consisted of four main kingdoms: East Anglia, Wessex, Northumbria and Mercia. Of these, Mercia was then the most powerful, militarily and economically, but in the later-9th century it was the kingdom of Wessex that was able to survive the attacks of the 'Great Army' (*Micel Here*), a motley collection of Scandinavian raiders who had all but destroyed the other three kingdoms during a decade of fighting.

To meet this problem, there was a gradual movement in the 9th century from undefended *wic* trading sites to trade taking place in defended sites, known in Old English as *burh*s. Urban fortifications such as those used in the burghal system were not a West Saxon innovation within either Anglo-Saxon England or Early Medieval Europe, but their systematic consolidation and regulation, probably under the system of administering fortifications recorded in the document known as the *Burghal Hidage*, may reflect the fact that it was Wessex, and the later kingdom of England under the West Saxon kings, which ensured that the defended urban site became an essential part of their success. Some 30 well-structured fortifications formed a framework of defence across the West Saxon heart of the Anglo-Saxon kingdom from the late-9th century onwards, a development that consolidated Alfred the Great's earlier victories.

However, some points of definition should be addressed at this stage. Although the work of many scholars would seem to suggest that it had assumed such a definition, the term *burh* did not mean a fortified town *per se*. Anglo-Saxons used the word to denote any place within a boundary, which could include private fortifications or simply a place with a hedge or fence around it. Indeed, the term *hage* simply meant boundary, so a 'hedge' may have been a fence rather than a line of trees and bushes, even if the distinction between the two may have been blurred by the fact that fences could resemble hedgerows if they were not attended to regularly. As one historian has pointed out, this term could even include the miserable existence of the kinless woman in the Anglo-Saxon poem *The Wife's Lament*, whose '*burh*' consisted simply of the brambles around the cave where she dwelt. Many *burhs* could also be privately occupied fortifications – in effect, early castles. Nevertheless, the organisation, administration and defence of the system of 'communal' fortifications designed as sites for a number of people in later Anglo-Saxon England, many of which became towns, are the main focus of this book.

Strictly speaking, 'Anglo-Saxon Wessex' refers to the historic shires (later counties) of Devon, Somerset, Wiltshire, Hampshire and Berkshire, which formed what has become known as the 'heartland' of the West Saxon kingdom. However, not least because of the dominance of the West Saxons over the areas of Sussex, Kent and Cornwall, the West Saxon kingdom gained hegemony over lowland Britain even before the Vikings became a major threat. Therefore, a consideration of Wessex here is a flexible one and reference will be made to those areas of Mercia south of the Danelaw boundary that fell into West Saxon hands as a result of victories against the Vikings in the late-9th and early-10th centuries.

Legend:
- Burghal Hidage sites with areas assigned (in hides)
- Royal estates named in King Alfred's will
- Roman roads

0   25 miles
0   50 km

GWYNEDD

POWYS

CEREDIGION

DYFED

BRYCHEINIOG

GWENT

GLYWYSING

ENGLISH MERCIA

DANISH MERCIA

EAST ANGLIA

WESSEX

ENGLISH CHANNEL

Alfred-Guthrum frontier c.880

Canterbury
Rochester
Southwark (1,800)
Beckley
Hastings (500)
Eastbourne
Beddingham
Lewes (1,300)
Rotherfield
Ditchling
Thunderfield
Alton
Leatherhead
Steyning
Beeding
Godalming
Eashing (600)
Guildford
Eashing
Angmering
Lyminster
Burpham
Crondall
Sutton
Candover
East Meon
Compton
Singleton
Aldingbourne
Felpham
Chichester (1,500)
Portchester (500)
Sutton
Arreton
Wellow
Sashes (1,000)
Wallingford (2,400)
Oxford (1,500)
Buckingham (1,600)
Wantage
Lambourn
Bedwyn
Kingsclere
Lower Hurstbourne
Winchester (2,400)
Dean
Wellow
Southampton (150)
Warwick (2,400)
Crickade (1,400)
Ashton Keynes
Chiseldon
Chisbury (700)
Hurstbourne
Amesbury
Christchurch (470)
Worcester (1,200)
Malmesbury (1,200)
Chippenham
Pewsey
Edington
Wilton (1,400)
Shaftesbury (700)
Sturminster
Wareham (1,600)
Bath (1,000)
Chewton
Yeovil
Bridport (760)
Whitchurch
Axbridge (400)
Wedmore
Crewkerne
Burnham
Langport (600)
Axmouth
Cannington
Lyng (100)
Cullompton
Branscombe
Watchet (513)
Kilton
Carhampton
Tiverton
Silverton
Exminster
Exeter (734)
Lustleigh
Halwell (300)
Lydford (140)
Pilton (400)
Lifton
Hartland
Stratton

Chronology

OPPOSITE The kingdom of Wessex and its neighbours. The map shows the 32 places which can be identified with varying levels of certainty in the *Burghal Hidage*, a document that dates from around 916 and records the amounts of land necessary for the maintenance of particular fortifications. Amongst various theories explored regarding the origins, purpose and nature of this document, it has been suggested that this may have been a 'paper exercise', designed to work out what would be needed for the maintenance of the West Saxon network of fortifications. The map also shows the relationship between the private resources of the West Saxon royal family, as shown in the will of King Alfred the Great, the communication network of Roman roads and trackways, and the 9th-century fortifications. Although there were other estates under royal control besides these shown in Alfred's will, the map still shows the importance of controlling the landscape, as envisaged by King Alfred.

Design and development

The early fortifications of Anglo-Saxon England

In the years that followed the Roman occupation, as western Romano-Celtic kingdoms and principalities emerged in parts of Britain, Iron Age hillforts became centres of power once more. Hillforts, such as that at South Cadbury, Somerset (most famously believed, among many other sites, to have been the site of King Arthur's Camelot), were a defining characteristic of the western Romano-Celtic kingdoms, which for some two centuries after the collapse of Roman central authority, identified themselves as 'different' from the invading English cultures. By contrast, the 'Anglo-Saxons' were not to develop their own fortifications for some centuries. In what was to become western Wessex, many sites lost their importance following the 7th-century extension of West Saxon influence beyond the River Parrett into western Somerset and Devon. While fortresses were not unknown to the early Anglo-Saxons, battles tended to be in the open and almost ritualistic in nature, with leaders being identified by treasure and the hall they provided.

Among the first fortifications in Anglo-Saxon England were those built in a linear fashion; these include earlier defences such as Devil's Dyke in East Anglia, Bokerley Dyke and Wansdyke in Wessex, which probably date to around the 6th century, and later ones such as Offa's Dyke, which established the Mercian kingdom's border with the Welsh kingdoms. Linear defences were intended to define the edges of kingdoms set up by conquest, prevent sporadic cattle raids and ensure that traders passing between territories paid tolls and taxes.

Early fortifications: Mercia

Offa's Dyke consisted of a series of 6ft-deep defensive ditches and 24ft-high ramparts that ran between the western frontier of the Mercian kingdom and the neighbouring Welsh kingdoms. A 9th-century Welsh bishop, Asser of St David's, writing at the West Saxon court of King Alfred, first recorded that King Offa of Mercia had built a 'great dyke' (*vallum magnum*) that ran 'from sea to sea' between his own kingdom and the kingdoms of his Welsh neighbours. Although the border between England and Wales fluctuated in later centuries, it is almost ironic that such an object of hostility (Offa's aggressive intentions can be seen in the surviving Welsh Annals, the *Annales Cambriae*) allowed the relative stability of Wales's only land border. However, there has been much dispute about the nature of the Dyke. While we have only Asser's attribution of the Dyke to King Offa, we can at least be reasonably sure that it was the product of an Anglo-Saxon Mercian kingdom at the height of its power, but other aspects are debated: did it, as some scholars have suggested, merely mark out a mutually agreed border between neighbouring kingdoms, or was it a monument of prestige in a manner similar to the marshalling of men and resources by prehistoric chieftains – simply undertaken in order to show that they were capable of such control? Alternatively, was it an Anglo-Saxon version of the Antonine or Hadrian's Wall, permanently garrisoned and ready for action in a distant frontier of the realm? There may be a tendency to believe that as effort and resources were invested in the construction of an effective linear defence, this could not have been for anything but military purposes. But while much of the Mercian kingdom may have been safe from Welsh attacks at this time, the garrisoning of the entire 150-mile (240km) frontier on a permanent basis in the manner of the more

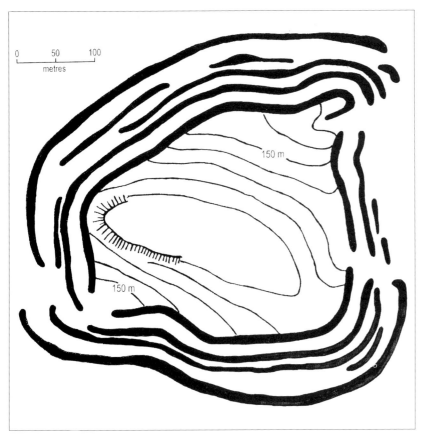

South Cadbury (Somerset): this was a multi-vallate hillfort dating from the Iron Age, which was pressed into use by a post-Roman British ruler of south-western territory. Due to an Antiquarian association of the nearby river Camel with the name 'Camelot' South Cadbury maintains 'Arthurian' adherents, but its tangible importance is that it is representative of a number of similar hillforts used for regional power in the post-Roman period (for its use in the late Anglo-Saxon period, see p.52). (Plan redrawn after L. Alcock, *Cadbury Castle*, 1995)

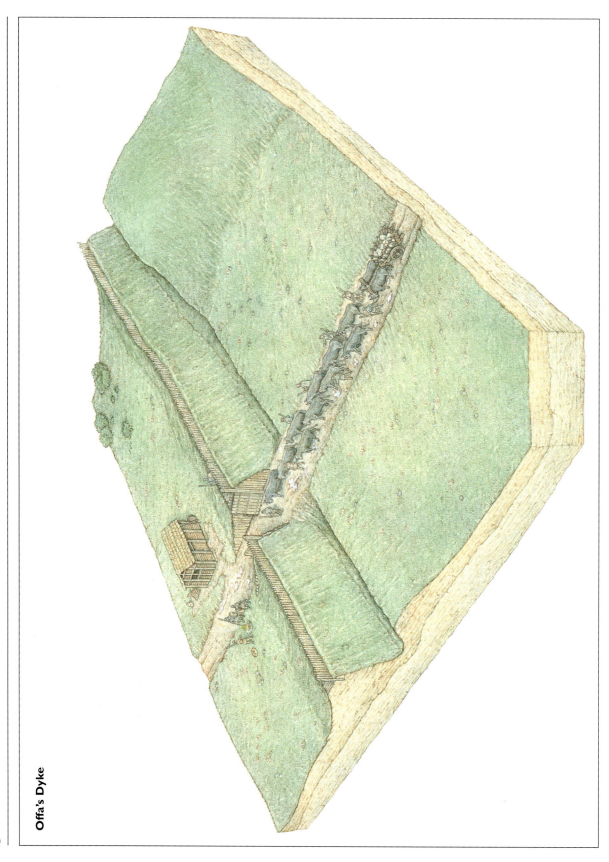

famous Roman defences may have been far beyond the means and resources of the Mercian kingdom.

The Dyke survives today for about 80 miles of its suggested course, but some questions remain unanswered regarding the significance of those areas where the Dyke does not survive. Its first modern surveyor, Sir Cyril Fox, postulated that the gaps represented those places where relations were least hostile with Welsh kingdoms, but more recent archaeological surveys have suggested that the 'gaps' were not intentional but rather reflect areas where the Dyke has not survived.

Equally, there is scepticism regarding the evidence for the provision of palisades to have been provided along the entire length of the Dyke. Although parts of the Dyke were near wooded areas, a 6ft-high palisade consisting of perhaps some half a million upright timbers, albeit only roughly worked, would have required the

Bokerley Dyke is one of the linear defences of early Wessex. It is notoriously difficult to provide reliable dating for large earthworks, but Bokerley Dyke is tentatively dated to the 6th century. Dykes such as these provided rulers with a defining line for the political control of territory. Such obviously impressive physical remains could have a long-lasting impact on the landscape; indeed Bokerley Dyke now forms part of the boundary between the modern counties of Hampshire and Dorset.

OPPOSITE **Offa's Dyke**

Offa's Dyke, Shropshire. The substantial archaeological remains bear out a 9th-century statement that King Offa of Mercia built a dyke that ran from sea to sea. Today, much of the fortification remains as earthworks, which still form the traditional border between Wales and England. Such linear types of fortification were prevalent in the early Anglo-Saxon period, although as the latest example of such, Offa's Dyke is also the most securely dated. The ditch and ramparts may have formed only a notional obstacle to any raiding party, but would have caused great difficulties for any attempt to return with any cattle raided, therefore addressing a major concern for the Anglo-Saxons of the area. It seems unlikely that the Dyke was intended to prevent the incursions of any substantial armies, but in the fact that the Mercian kingdom remained safe upon its western borders, it appears to have done its job. As the height from bottom of ditch to top of rampart could be as much as 24ft (8m),

this was more than a simple boundary marker. Historians and archaeologists have addressed the length of time and work that may have been invested in the construction of the Dyke and it is suggested that the variations in construction along different stretches of the fortification may have been a result of the work of different gangs of labourers working during successive building seasons. Along some of the length of the Dyke earthen ramparts may have been surmounted by a wooden palisade, but in other places the ditch and ramparts may have been considered to have sufficed. Here, cattle are driven along one of the ancient drove roads passing through one of the Dyke's entrances. Although it is suggested that the fortification could not be permanently manned in the same manner as Hadrian's Wall, as the Mercian kingdom could hardly afford to support a standing army, it is hardly conceivable that passageways through the Dyke would not have had some soldiers standing guard, with the consequent benefits of toll payments.

The course of Offa's Dyke, along the border between western Mercia and the Welsh kingdoms. The Dyke survives in about 80 miles of its suggested 140-mile course. In some places the Dyke used the natural topography of the landscape such as ranges of hills to emphasise the barrier that it provided. (Redrawn after D. Hill, *Atlas of Anglo-Saxon England*, 1981)

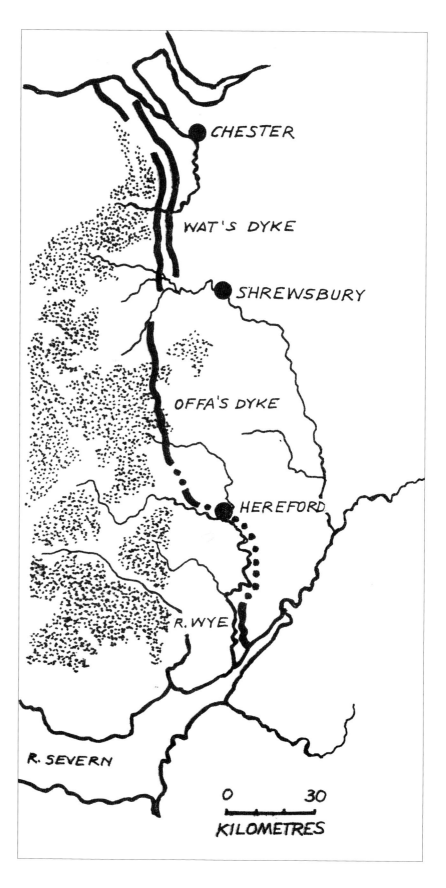

CHESTER

WAT'S DYKE

SHREWSBURY

OFFA'S DYKE

HEREFORD

R. WYE

R. SEVERN

0   30
KILOMETRES

felling of hundreds of thousands of trees, as well as an extravagant amount of labour to fell, work and emplace them. Even if a high proportion of this work was unskilled, this would still have been a massive drain on resources already stretched by the need to mobilise labour gangs for the construction of the ditches and ramparts. At those points where the border traffic may have been heavy, generally where ancient trackways crossed the Dyke, it may be logical to suggest that some attention was paid to crowning the ramparts with palisades and providing guards in order to ensure that dues and tolls were paid and that the Dyke maintained a formidable presence.

Whatever the techniques used in its construction, however, this does not undermine the achievement of the king and his administrators in gathering together the Dyke. Although it was hardly a Hadrian's Wall – there is no evidence of anything resembling milecastles, for instance – it may still have been an important defence against potential invading armies, an effective device for taxing trade and no doubt also a symbol of the prestige of the Mercian king.

In addition to Offa's Dyke, the Mercian kingdom was also the first of the Anglo-Saxon kingdoms to introduce fortified settlements in the form of *burhs*. Evidence from charters recording the granting of land to churches reveals 8th-century Mercia to have been the most forward thinking of the Anglo-Saxon kingdoms, ensuring that military service was incorporated into the services available to the kingdom. Charters reserved the rights of the king to claim work in a threefold manner: on bridges (*bricgweorc*), the army (*fyrdweorc*), and fortifications (*burhweorc*), all of which would be provided by the owner of the land. In some cases, monetary contributions may have been made rather than the actual provision of manpower, but Mercian rulers had become more advanced than the Northumbrian rulers of the time who, with zealous piety, had granted too much land to establish monasteries and, as a result, were unable to command military services from the lands that they had granted. In Mercia, the king was able to 'reserve' the military services due to him. With Mercian influence so prevalent in 8th-century England, it is perhaps unsurprising that Wessex soon followed suit in ensuring that military services were provided by ecclesiastical and monastic landholders.

Early West Saxon defences

Far from being introduced into Wessex by Alfred the Great, as is often assumed, it has been suggested by Nicholas Brooks that 'communal' fortifications in the form of *burhs* had been built since at least the early-9th century, when West Saxon charters were stringent in recording the obligations of fortification-work. Furthermore, the *Anglo-Saxon Chronicle* contains a record of a late-8th-century battle in a fortification of some kind – described as a *byrig* – between two rival members of the West Saxon royal house, King Cynewulf and his kinsman Cyneheard. This may suggest that small private fortifications existed at least some 50 years before *burhs* were used as 'communal' fortifications. The entry shows that the West Saxon king was meeting his mistress in what is usually interpreted as a bower or a large manor house at *Meretun*. The rebellious *aetheling*, Cyneheard, entered the *byrig* and cut down his kinsman, King Cynewulf. The king's warrior retinue, sleeping in another part of the complex, were woken by the woman's screams. The usurper offered rich rewards to the king's retinue if only they would support him, but they refused and, so we are told, fought on to die gloriously.

Here was the ideal of Anglo-Saxon aristocratic society. The suggestion that no man would support the usurper, but all would fight for their dead lord was at least a literary ideal that was well understood, even to the audience of the poem of the *Battle of Maldon* two centuries later. This chronicle entry, which is suggested to reflect the oral transmission of a historical event, is unusually detailed and supplies evidence for the layout of an aristocratic hall with its central sleeping quarters for the lord (the entry does not inform us whether it was the king or his mistress who actually owned the property) and a separate building for the king's companions. Furthermore, the record of the reprisal raid upon the newly captured *Meretun* suggests that this was also fortified:

> In the morning, when the king's thegns who had been left behind heard that the king was slain, they rode there ... and found the *ætheling* in the *byrig* where the king lay slain, and they had closed the gates against them ... And then he promised them their own choice of money and land if they would allow him the kingdom; and he reminded them that their kinsmen were with him and would not desert him. They replied to him that no kinsman was dearer to them than their lord, and they never would follow his slayer ... And they carried on fighting around the gates until they rushed in, and they slew the *ætheling* and the men who were with him, all except one.

The arguing and bargaining between the different forces outside the fortification reflects the divisions that rent the kingdom in what was essentially a civil war. However, it is the closing of the gates that should concern us here, as a motif that was used in other *Anglo-Saxon Chronicle* entries to signify the defence of a fortification. Clearly this was a fortified site and battle raged both outside and, when the situation grew more desperate, inside.

Although *Meretun* remains unidentified, the defence of a lord's hall is identifiable as a feature of early Anglo-Saxon warrior psychology, evidenced by the fragment of poetry known as the *Fight at Finnsburh*, written from an event in a distantly remembered past, in which a group of warriors defend a hall for five days and nights. Although the site itself was probably in Frisia (now in the Netherlands), the Anglo-Saxon society that retold the story thought of a lord's hall as a place to be defended bravely. Even the *Beowulf* poem, which includes a bard's retelling of the *Finnsburh* battle, has at its heart the defence of the lord's hall by the king's men. Although, as a number of historians have noted, Anglo-Saxon battles may have been fought at mutually agreed times and places in an almost ritualistic manner, there was still room for attacks on places of residence.

If the followers of the early Anglo-Saxon kings were fed and protected (and, in return, protected the kings) in their kings' halls, then it follows that, as kings

The lid of the Franks Casket, dating from the 8th century, depicting a character by the name of Egil defending his home against an attack. Although of Northumbrian provenance, this scene shows the manner in which the defence of a hall (and within it the lord's kindred and followers) was a highly important aspect of Anglo-Saxon society. (Courtesy of the Trustees of the British Museum)

developed control of wider realms and greater populations, thus increasing the sophistication of the means by which they could gain wealth, they needed larger protected spaces.

Alfred the Great

For the systematic management of this, King Alfred the Great may be given a great deal of the credit. The middle and later years of the 9th century saw the increased and regular development of *burhs* as large fortified urban areas within the West Saxon kingdom as well as in Mercia. In the early-9th century this had been a type of defence that was not yet systematised and was probably designed primarily against the threat of small groups of Viking raiders who had been active in the English kingdoms in significant numbers since at least the 820s, if not before.

However, as with so many Anglo-Saxon achievements, it is to the European continent and the Carolingian Franks that we should turn in order to see the spur behind the development of a systematic defensive arrangement similar to the *Burghal Hidage*. By the 860s Charles the Bald had organised western Francia, now modern-day France, to finance a system of fortified bridges across the River Seine in order to block the passage of Viking invaders. Given the penchant of King Alfred for introducing Frankish institutions into his own kingdom the West Saxon *burhs* are likely to have been an equivalent. Although there were certainly fortifications in Anglo-Saxon England before the reign of Charles the Bald in Francia, the systematic design and administration of the fortifications may well have been a Frankish import.

The significance of systematically administering fortifications may have been brought home to Alfred following his refuge at Athelney in the Somerset Levels in 878. Asser probably described Alfred as making a 'fortress' (*fecit arcem*) at Athelney because it was in a naturally advantageous position and needed little to improve it. While most military encounters in the campaigns of 871–78 had taken place in the open it had been the Vikings who took the strategic advantage, in terms of seizing and often fortifying defensible sites. In the campaigns leading up to the battle of Edington (Wilts.), the Iron Age fortress of

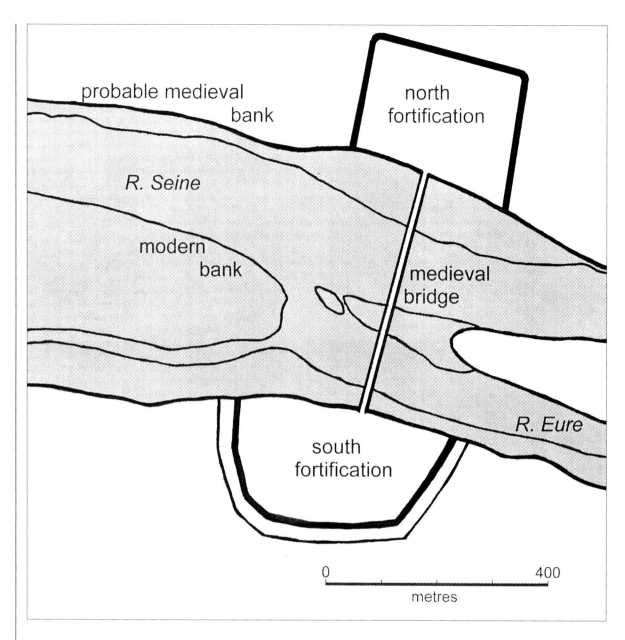

probable medieval bank

R. Seine

modern bank

north fortification

medieval bridge

R. Eure

south fortification

0   400

metres

A Frankish 'double-borough', built during the reign of King Charles the Bald in the middle years of the 9th century. Although Charles suffered a large number of Viking raids during his reign, contrary to popular belief, he was able to maintain a defence of his kingdom by the use of such fortifications controlling the crossing points of rivers, a strategy which Alfred the Great was to follow to his advantage in Wessex. (Redrawn after J. M. Hassall and D. Hill, 'Pont de l'Arche: Frankish Influence on the West Saxon Burh?', *Archaeological Journal*, 127, 1970)

Bratton Camp may have served as a base for the Vikings, and they later took refuge in the West Saxon fortification of Chippenham, the siege of which lasted two weeks until the Vikings were starved into submission.

The decisive defeat of the Vikings at Edington in 878 gave the West Saxon king an opportunity to undertake wide-ranging military reforms of the kingdom in order to consolidate its defence; these reforms included increasing the available manpower for the army and the provision of a naval force, as well as, most significantly for the purposes of this book, the supply and garrisoning of fortifications. This system meant the building of some new fortresses in order to ensure that no part of the kingdom was more than a day's travel (20 miles) from a fortification. While the system is sometimes interpreted as the provision of refuge for the peasants of the countryside there was more to it than this. The *burhs* could also be used offensively, allowing mounted forces based within the garrisons to pursue Viking raiders in their locality and ensuring that large enough forces could be brought to bear upon any threat.

In its entry for 893, the *Anglo-Saxon Chronicle* describes how Alfred 'divided his army into two, so that half its men were always at home, and half on service, apart from those men who guarded the *burhs*'. Such a precise division of manpower may have been a literary embellishment, but it also seemed to be a sensible division of labour and other entries in the *Chronicle* suggest that armed forces may even have been permanently based within *burhs*. Even if the military obligations were limited to freemen (excepting slaves and the lower orders of peasantry), this was an enormous burden for the kingdom to bear. It has been suggested that in the early Middle Ages it took three peasants to supply the surplus food needed for one purely non-agricultural worker. Furthermore, the need to bring fortifications up to an effective condition and maintain them meant the digging of ditches, the repairing of stone walls, the construction of new earthworks, cutting roads, felling of trees and construction of palisades to a level that had not been seen in southern England since the time of the Roman occupation.

The other important record that describes the organisation of the defences of the West Saxon kingdom, as well as their locations, is known as the *Burghal Hidage*. Hides were a measure of land assessment, which were roughly 120 acres each in Wessex, and the *Burghal Hidage* set out these areas of land intended for the administration of each *burh*, which varied from small assessments such as 150 hides for Southampton, to such massive assessments as Winchester's 2,400 hides. Even if we should not place all our faith in the *Burghal Hidage* as a comprehensive

Athelney, Wessex; the 'noble island' in the Somerset Levels that King Alfred used as his base against the Vikings in 878. Although ditches dug in the 19th century drained the Levels, much of the area in the Middle Ages was flooded marshland, impassable to those who did not know it. The naturally raised ground of Athelney, visible here in this photograph (the monument was built in the 19th century to commemorate Alfred's victory), meant that it provided an important refuge. (Photograph by Don Lavelle)

description of the defences of Wessex, as such defensible and obviously important sites such as Canterbury, Rochester (both Kent) and Dorchester (Dorset) are not mentioned in it, it at least gives some sense of the administration necessary to build and maintain the network of defences in Wessex.

The total assessment came to 27,000 hides across the West Saxon kingdom. Due to the *Burghal Hidage*'s record of certain towns contributing to the defence of the kingdom, the document in its existing form probably does not date from the reign of King Alfred, but from the reign of his son Edward the Elder, who consolidated the achievements of his father by extending the influence of the West Saxon kingdom into the southern midlands. Therefore, Warwick, Buckingham and Worcester appear in the document, though these may also be interpolations entered into an earlier document. However, the organisation that lay behind the *Burghal Hidage* is generally accepted to have been the work of Alfred the Great. An appendix to the *Burghal Hidage* presents a calculation by which the assessments may have been reached:

> For the foundation of a wall of one acre's breadth, and for its defence, 16 hides are needed. If each hide is manned by one man, then each pole may be worked by four men.

These were logical calculations and although they may simply have been theoretical, as some historians have recently suggested, they at least show that administrators were dealing with the taxing subject of how the kingdom (a newly enlarged kingdom in the 910s, when the existing document was compiled) could be defended.

There is some disagreement among scholars as to whether the authors of the *Burghal Hidage* were calculating the resources that they had available and tailoring the allocation of defences accordingly or were setting out the resources necessary for the defences of the existing *burhs*. It has been noted that the totals of land in the *Burghal Hidage* are surprisingly similar to the assessments in Domesday Book, so perhaps the administrators were working with calculable resources in order to set out the defences of the *burhs*.

Although larger fortifications were obviously more effective in resisting attack, the kingdom could not rely upon investing its resources in a small number of large fortifications, as this would have meant that some areas would not have been within reach of a fortification. The *Burghal Hidage* shows that a balance had to be struck; even if some of the smaller fortifications which it records were too small to be efficiently supported by the kingdom's pool of manpower and supplies, and were later to fall out of use, in the short term they played a vital part in maintaining the integrity of the network of defence across the kingdom.

The *Burghal Hidage* formula has also led to historians and archaeologists undertaking numerous calculations in order to ascertain – with varying amounts of success – the sizes of the fortifications, as the hidage attributed to a site could then lead to the calculation of the length of the walls. In the case of Winchester, the calculations are remarkably accurate; the theoretical calculation of 3,300yds that can be reached from Winchester's 2,400 hides equates almost perfectly with the Roman walls' actual length of 3,317yds. In recent years, the *Burghal Hidage* has also been useful for discovering the layout of the *burh* at Christchurch (*Twynham*, Hants, now Dorset), where no remains of the defences survive above ground. Its measurement of 470 hides, equating to 646yds, meant that, using street plans, archaeologists were able to ascertain the location of some of the defences. However, on other occasions the *Burghal Hidage* appears to have had less correspondence with surviving fortifications, such as at Lydford, where the calculation may only equate to one wall's worth of fortification, or Wareham, where the *Burghal Hidage* equates with three of the four walls. This has led to the suggestion that the document was not necessarily an official statement of policy

Construction of a *burh*

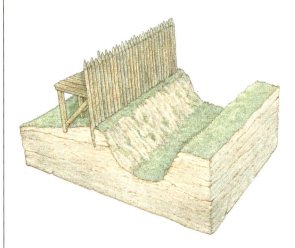
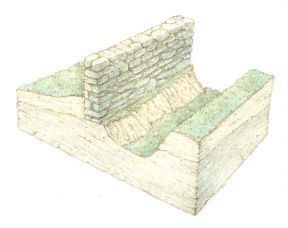

Excavations have suggested that wooden structures were used to give stability to the high earthen ramparts that provided a key element of the defences. The conjectural reconstruction provided here, following other contemporary European forms of fortification, allows the underlying structure to form part of the fighting platform. Other forms of providing stability to a defensive rampart were the use of turf walls or the use of a well-made facing stone wall (although the latter seems less likely in the first phases of the construction of a network of defences, and probably belonged to a phase of consolidation of the defences during a period in which there may have been less immediate threat). Timber revetments may have been constructed to give stability to the earthen ramparts while they settled and,

along with the rampart palisades, could have presented an impressive continuous face. However, there appears to have been no single design for the construction of ramparts and local variations may have also included the use of fire-hardened up-ended stakes to form a more rudimentary palisade. The peasantry of the West Saxon countryside were impressed into the work on the fortifications. On the right, a group are digging the defensive ditch, the earth from which is being moved to form the rampart. Fire-hardened stakes have been radially split along their lengths and placed into a trench to form a palisade that also acts as a revetment. Behind, it is probable that larger fortifications had fighting platforms in order to allow the benefit of height to the defenders.

The layout of the walls of the *burh* at *Twynham* (Christchurch), now in Dorset but formerly in Hampshire. The length and layout of the walls have been calculated through a comparison of the *Burghal Hidage*'s theoretical length of the walls against a plan of the town and excavations have found evidence of turf earthworks, later faced with stone, along these lines. The marshy floodplain produced by the rivers Stour and Avon may have meant that substantial walls were only required on the northern and southern sides of the town. (Redrawn after Hill and Rumble, *Defence of Wessex*)

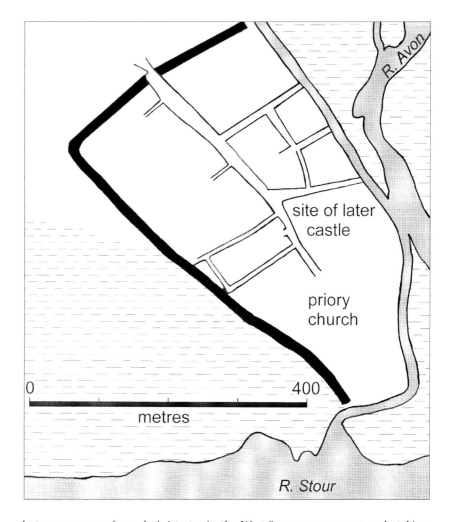

but more a case of an administrator in the West Saxon government undertaking calculations with official and accurate figures for the administration of the kingdom. With Domesday Book's figures correlating with such accuracy, we might therefore be able to make some sense of the *Anglo-Saxon Chronicle*'s statement on the proportion of West Saxon men in burghal service. Nicholas Brooks has suggested that the 27,000 men involved in the defence of the kingdom may have represented a proportion of as much as one in five or six of the able-bodied male population. Even allowing for the inevitable discrepancies between levels of conscription and reality, this is still a remarkable level, equalled only by the large national armies of the Early Modern period, thus suggesting that the fortification of the kingdom was an important part of royal policy at the end of the 9th century and the beginning of the 10th.

'Private' fortifications: Anglo-Saxon castles?

While the *byrig* recorded in a battle at *Meretun* in the *Anglo-Saxon Chronicle* discussed above may be a rare piece of evidence for small fortifications, there is an increasing awareness of a number of small fortifications in private ('thegnly') hands from the 10th century onwards. This may have been a result of what appears to have been a developing trend in this period, of private landholding. Such developments in private fortification may provide a contrast (even if a somewhat artificial distinction) to the decline in a system of garrisoned *burh*s, which had become more associated with mints and markets than with their palisades or ramparts.

Site	Hides assigned to site	Theoretical length of walls (m)	Actual/estimated length of walls (m)
Axbridge	400	503	?
Bath	1,000	1,257	1,143
Bridport	760	956	?
Buckingham	1,600	2012	?
Burpham	720	905	?
Chichester	1500	1,886	2,377
Chisbury	700	880	994
Christchurch	470	591	610
Cricklade	1,500	1,886	2,073
Eashing	600	754	?
Eorpeburnan	324	407	?
Exeter	734	923	2,316
Halwell	300	377	366
Hastings	500	629	?
Langport	600	754	?
Lewes	1,200	1,509	?
Lydford	140	176	311
Lyng	100	126	171
Malmesbury	1,200	1,509	1,320
Oxford	1,500	1,886	1,840
Pilton	360	453	?
Portchester	500	629	637
Sashes	1,000	1,257	?
Shaftesbury	700	880	?
Southampton	150	189	?
Southwark	1,800	2,263	?
Wallingford	2,400	3,018	2,830
Wareham	1,600	2,012	1,993
Warwick	2,400	3,018	1,524
Watchet	513	645	?
Wilton	1,400	1,760	?
Winchester	2,400	3,018	3,034
Worcester	1,200	1,509	1,417

The statistics of the *Burghal Hidage*. Following a principle observed by David Hill, a calculation is possible for the theoretical lengths of wall needed for each fortification according to the *Burghal Hidage's* formula of just over 3ft of wall per hide. In a few cases, where 'actual' lengths of wall can be discerned, they compare remarkably well with the 'theoretical' lengths. Were these an 'ideal' by which the formula had originally been calculated?

There is some question as to whether the private fortifications were integrated into the 'national' system of defence or whether they were simply the manifestations of private wealth shown off through the building of castles, as happened in parts of France. Anglo-Saxon thegns, however, had bonds of duties to the king that manifested themselves to a greater degree than the French nobility. Therefore, it is worth considering the few private fortifications found in later Anglo-Saxon England as examples of part of a defensive network, even if this was not as strong as the earlier system provided by King Alfred. While the fortifications may have been paid for by the private wealth of a few individuals

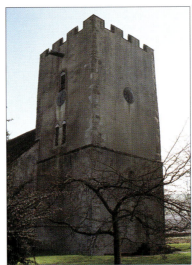

Examples of substantial late Anglo-Saxon stone towers attached to churches at Bosham and Singleton in Sussex, and St Michael's church, Oxford. Of the three, Bosham is the least likely to have been used in any fortification context, as the nave of the church against which it stands also dates from the same period. However, Bosham is a good example of the way in which a church and private hall could be almost synonymous as Earl Harold Godwineson famously stopped at the church on his estate on his way to Normandy c. 1064. The tower at Bosham provided an important navigation point for ships sailing along Bosham Channel and therefore may also have supplied a vantage point for the observation of incoming ships. St Michael's church in Oxford stands on the line of the medieval city walls and may have provided some form of defence or vantage point, while Singleton church tower, although partly restored after a 17th-century lightning strike, may have formed part of a manorial complex (the crenellations are not Anglo-Saxon).

rather than by the national wealth (as was the case with the communal *burh*s), the private fortifications may have provided adequate defences in parts of the countryside in the 10th and 11th centuries.

A document from the 11th century records the manner in which a *ceorl* (a high-status peasant) had needed a gate, tower and church in order to ascend to thegnly status:

> And if a *ceorl* prospered, so that he had fully five hides of his own land, a church and kitchen, a bell-house and *burh*-gate, a seat and special office in the king's hall, thenceforth he was worthy of thegnly rank.

Although inadequate as a record of the legal status of the thegn, it does at least suggest that in the 'old days', at which the author of the document (probably Wulfstan, Archbishop of York) looked back with wistful nostalgia, the identity of a thegn was very much based upon his holding of a private, fortified hall.

The survival of stone towers has led to the identification of 'thegnly residences', dating from the 10th and 11th centuries. A number of these survive with the addition of later church buildings in parts of England. While the assumption that a structure may have always stood as a church may be logical, it does not necessarily seem have to have been the case. Architectural historians and archaeologists have suggested that such towers

OPPOSITE **Private fortification**
A private fortification of a thegn. An 11th-century document recorded that a man would be entitled to the rights of a thegn if he had a *burh*-gate, a bell, a church and a seat in the king's hall. This may have been rather too rigid as a definition of social mobility, but it nonetheless gives an indication that small fortifications were constructed in the later Anglo-Saxon period and held on a private basis. Such fortifications may have been a far cry from the larger castles built in post-Conquest England by the great Anglo-Norman magnates, but there does appear to have been some similarity between such small private Anglo-Saxon fortifications and the lesser castles in England and Normandy. A palisade may have been an indicator of the

area under the lord's control and hardly provided a stout defence against an attacking army, but such residential complexes were inherently concerned with the status of the aristocrat who owned them rather than with defence. It has been suggested by some scholars that towers may have been an important part of such a complex; while perhaps also fulfilling a religious function and an efficient means of observation, they were also important in order to show the lord's position of control over the countryside. As this scene shows, the local peasants knew that they had to come to the lord's manor, which fulfilled many of the same functions as the later castle. By at least the 10th century, the division of the landscape, a process more often associated with the Norman Conquest, had already begun.

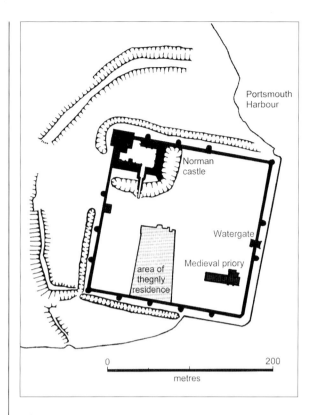

Portchester, Hampshire, a Roman shore fortress converted in the later Anglo-Saxon period into, first, a *burh* for the local community, then a 'thegnly residence', with a high-status hall building in one corner of the complex. The 'Watergate', which has been suggested to date from the 11th century, may have been part of the local lord's investment in the site. (Redrawn after B. Cunliffe, *Excavations at Portchester Castle*, 1976)

may have had a secular function at some point and been incorporated into the building of a later church nave. While such later church towers may also have been part of the defences of cities (for example St Michael's church on the city walls of Oxford), it is as status symbols for the lord of the manor that towers, whether built from stone or timber, may also have been built. Standing high above the countryside and the estate, they projected the importance of the lord who had built them. Given the earlier reference to a *burh*-gate (*burhgeat*), it has also been suggested that the tower may have served some function as a gateway into a fortified residential complex, which included a grand hall and probably also a church building. The '*burh*' in *burhgeat* may have been a reference to the entranceway to a fortification, or indeed may have implied that the entrance itself was fortified.

The thegnly residence excavated at Portchester (Hants.) blurs the boundaries between 'private' and 'communal' fortifications, as it was a former Roman shore fort that was recorded as a part of the burghal system of Alfred the Great. Perhaps this had been the case since the beginning of the 10th century, when a charter was drawn up to record the king's exchange of land from elsewhere in order to take this strategic coastal land from the Bishop of Winchester. Although the magnificent Norman castle that occupies one corner of the complex attracts a great deal of attention, the archaeologist who excavated the site noted that a high-status, probably lordly residence was a key feature of the 10th/11th-century Anglo-Saxon phase of occupation. This may coincide with the building of the 'Watergate', a stone gateway that formed the entrance to this part of the complex.

Portchester is an interesting example of a communal fortification that may have become downgraded within the defensive network of Wessex in later years. Fortified thegnly residences may have provided a stone tower in the centre of the complex, with a large gateway showing the importance given to the entrance. The palisades and ramparts may have been rudimentary by comparison with post-Conquest castles and the towers would have been unable to withstand any siege equipment of the sort that military technology would later provide. However, that was not the point. Even though their chief purpose may have been to display the status, wealth and even a certain degree of independence of their owner, they would still have presented an obstacle to any raiding party. Furthermore, they would have provided some means of dominating the local countryside in the types of rivalries that manifested themselves in later Anglo-Saxon England.

Fortifications in the landscape

In addition to ensuring that no part of the kingdom was more than 20 miles from a fortification, the network of fortifications provided protection for the central points across the West Saxon landscape. It was necessary to meet the threats to the economy posed by the Viking armies, who in assaults on other Anglo-Saxon kingdoms, and in Wessex in the early 870s, had focused upon attacking the centres of royal estates in order to seize the royal food renders (*feorm*) that had been gathered there. The 'year of the nine battles' (871) had seen the Viking army attacking a number of royal estates and this may have been particularly instrumental in forcing the new West Saxon king Alfred to realise the vulnerability of the central resources within his kingdom. If Viking invaders had access to the means of wealth available to a king then they could effectively control the kingdom itself. The tragedy of the situation in the *Beowulf* poem, where the aged king could not entertain his retainers in the hall at Heorot because of the fear of the monster Grendel, may have resonated with King Alfred's own experience, and the message may have come home to him as he and his followers were attacked in midwinter at Chippenham in 878. The king's resources, his food and the revenues from his estates, and indeed the very people who worked those estates needed protection.

Therefore, the burghal system had to be ready and able to collect the food produced at harvest times, and so these fortifications became central places in the agricultural economy. One of the primary purposes of the fortifications was to protect and administer the local economy, and the fact that no Viking incursions into Wessex were successful for at least a century after 878 is at least in some small part a measure of their success.

However, the strategic thinking that lay behind the construction of the *burh*s was more than simply the creation of an armoured shell around the existing structure of the countryside. The *burh*s were integrated into a landscape of defence, controlling the nodes of communication and allowing armies to move quickly along roads that were maintained for the use of armies. These were the so-called 'army roads' or *herepaths* – it may be that as *here* tended to refer to invading armies rather than defensive ones, the *herepath* was therefore a road for use against the *here*. The roads may have been useful in allowing the population of the countryside to reach shelter quickly in the face of an attacking Viking army, but they were also instrumental in allowing a form of 'offensive defence' to take place. If, as Alfred intended, a garrison was present in each of the *burh*s, the intricate network of fortifications and road communication allowed the West Saxons to gather an army, often from more than one *burh*, to the area and defeat an invading Viking force. If the well-maintained roads allowed a mounted Viking force to move more swiftly than they might otherwise have done, as may have happened when Vikings travelled up and down Wessex in 1006, then, at least in theory, there would have been a force at hand to meet the invaders. This meant that a mounted force presumably had to be ready for action quickly (at least in times of war). We may perhaps gather that the forces from two neighbouring fortresses would have been able to bring a large combined force together, with a maximum radius of operations of perhaps 30 miles, within about half a day. A Viking force could cause a great deal of damage in such a time but, in spreading out to cause such damage, it would also be vulnerable; with luck, the very presence of the fortifications and the forces ready to attack an invading force from fortifications would deter that invading force from causing too much damage.

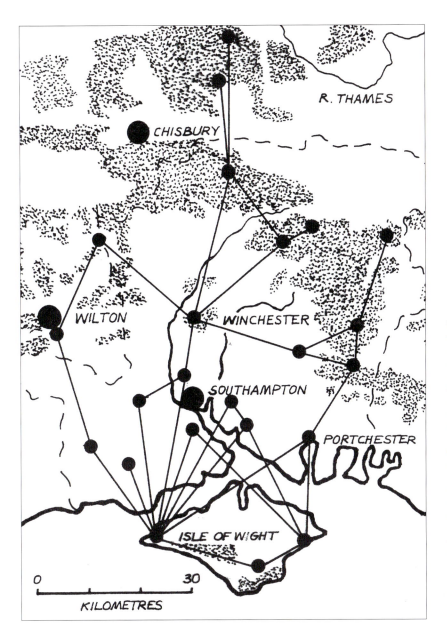

The warning system connected to the fortifications of the kingdom also added another dimension to defence, as shown in this system reconstructed by David Hill for Hampshire. High points of land are sometimes recorded in Anglo-Saxon land boundary records as 'beacons'; Beacon Hill (left), near Highclere, overlooking much of northern Hampshire, is so-called because of its importance as a signal point against the 16th-century Armada, but in a late Anglo-Saxon charter recording a grant of land in this area the hill is recorded as providing the same role some five centuries earlier. Silbury Hill (right), near Avebury in Wiltshire, is a famous prehistoric monument, but archaeological excavations have also suggested that it may have been used as a signal point in the late Anglo-Saxon period.

It has been argued, with some justification, that the network of fortifications was also connected by a series of beacons ready to be lit upon the approach of an invading army. Anglo-Saxon charter boundaries record the presence of beacon fires on some high ground (indeed the word 'beacon' itself is Old English). A beacon system has been reconstructed in Hampshire, based upon that designed in the 16th century to warn of the approach of the Spanish Armada. Given the similarities of the situation with that of the late Anglo-Saxon period, it is a logical deduction to make. After all, Wessex had an undulating landscape with a number of high points from which the surrounding area could be made out. For example, on a clear day it is possible to see both the Isle of Wight in the Solent and Beacon Hill in the north of Hampshire from the top of Meon Hill near the centre of the county. Of course, the Anglo-Saxons may not have wished to rely upon clear weather, but with multiple visual connections from each beacon the system would have continued to function even if one fire was not maintained.

On the face of it, a beacon warning system may appear crude but, as with the building of large earthworks, it was not so much the essential basic design that was sophisticated or otherwise, rather the fact that these beacons were part of an extensive network of defence. Keeping a woodpile dry and ready to be lit in time of possible attack (which arguably could come at any time), ensuring that there was a signalling system able to take into account different messages and making sure that there were at least two people alert and watchful enough to be able to light the beacons would have been no mean feat.

Roads are also recorded in a number of boundary clauses in charters recording grants of land in Wessex. Almost verbal maps for walking from point to point on the boundary of a piece of land, the charter bounds provide useful pieces of evidence to show the division of the landscape, and while a number of such roads were re-used Roman roads or even prehistoric trackways, others had been newly constructed by the West Saxon state itself. This may have been included in part of the expenditure upon which King Alfred had placed so much faith. As we have seen, the Anglo-Saxon charters recorded payments for *burh*-work, army-work and bridgework. Arguably, the maintenance of the roads was included in this.

A similar degree of civil engineering may have applied to the construction of bridges. Twenty-two of the 33 fortifications named in the *Burghal Hidage* were at river crossings, even if not all of them necessarily incorporated bridges. Although the fortifications of the western Franks have been termed 'fortified bridges', there is unlikely to have been much difference between these and the West Saxon defences at river crossings. It has been suggested that the bridges themselves were not so much fortified as providing a potential barrier to river-borne traffic, forcing attacking Vikings to travel by land, where they would be vulnerable to attack from garrisons based within the fortification.

Five of the remaining 10 *burhs* – Hastings (Sussex), Portchester, Southampton (both Hampshire), Christchurch (*Twynham*, now Dorset) and Watchet (Somerset) – controlled coastal areas. Arguably, Exeter and Chichester could also be included in such assessment as they were close to the coast. Along with the newly built ships that King Alfred pressed into service in the defence of Wessex, such coastal fortifications show the importance that was placed upon the control of maritime navigation. While we cannot judge whether such sites were the bases for the Alfredian navy we can at least assume that such sites were intended to deny coastal regions to Viking raiders, thus giving the Anglo-Saxon naval forces the opportunity to catch up. Arguably, this very thing happened in the last known military action undertaken by King Alfred in 896, when a force of Vikings attacked the Isle of Wight rather than the better-defended Hampshire mainland, although it should be added that on this occasion the West Saxon naval pursuit of the pirates was somewhat unsuccessful.

Of the remaining six *burhs*, Pilton and *Eorpburnan* are identified only speculatively, but may have been constructed from former Iron Age hillforts.

Those sites that we know were not by, or close to, rivers were set up in high places or in marshy areas, as is the case for Lyng (Somerset), which was connected by a causeway to Athelney to create a 'double *burh*'.

The principles of defence

If the wider strategic considerations of defence within the landscape were subtle, the immediate defence of a *burh* under attack may have been less so. In the event of an attack, the defence of the *burh* and its inhabitants depended upon bringing a force to bear against the attackers. This was probably an extension of the land warfare practiced at the time: arrows shot at a distant enemy, spears thrown as they approached and, finally, bringing as many warriors to bear as possible upon any enemy who managed to breach the ramparts.

The *Burghal Hidage* document shows the area of wall that was to be defended by one man as just over 3ft. This was arguably the area of space taken up by one man in the 'shieldwall'. Therefore, if, as has been suggested, the *Burghal Hidage* was a 'paper exercise' intended to calculate the resources necessary for the defence of the kingdom, then the principle that warriors stood almost shoulder to shoulder upon the battlefield may have been the most logical comparison to make in order to calculate this.

However, the idea that one man occupied 3ft of wall in its defence was obviously not put forward for modern military historians to take literally! It may not even have represented an ideal but rather a point of departure from which calculations could be made. Each of the defenders may not have been expected to occupy an equal space upon the palisades during the period of an attack, but it is important to remember that in times of attacks upon them, the *burh*s were intended to act as force multipliers, to delay an attack so that the forces from neighbouring garrisons could come to their aid. On some occasions, such as the Londoners' ill-advised charge out of their fortified walls

King Alfred's biographer, Asser, records that the *burh* of Lyng was connected to the monastery at Athelney by means of a causeway across the marshes. As it was a substantial roadway designed to allow the passage of a high volume of traffic, the Athelney–Lyng causeway across the Somerset Levels may have been of a similar pattern to the 700m bridge built at Ravninge Enge in Denmark (Jutland) in the 10th century, consisting of 4m piles driven into the marshy ground at regular intervals, after which this reconstruction is based. (Drawing by Don Lavelle)

'Generic' West Saxon *burh*

A reconstruction of a typical West Saxon *burh*, giving details of a number of points of urban life and military defence in later Anglo-Saxon Wessex. The fortification represented here shows the different types of wall and rampart, and represents the transition of construction from wood to stone.

1 Large 'minster' church
2 Parish church
3 Surviving Roman wall, used in the fortification's ramparts
4 Wooden palisade
5 Construction of a new stone wall
6 Internal road, running along the course of the ramparts; their defensive purposes were for the rapid movement of forces within the *burh*
7 Bridge; constructed from wood, this could also have protected the site from riverborne attackers
8 High-status manorial building
9 Private, 'lordly' church, belonging to the manor
10 Main gateway; constructed from stone
11 Smaller gateways
12 Traders' market
13 Defensive tower
14 Mounted thegns; the offensive strike-force provided by West Saxon fortifications
15 Trading ship at quayside
16 Construction of new buildings in wood and stone
17 A group of workers preparing mortar for stone construction
18 Blacksmith's workshop
19 Small fields of crops just outside the town walls, showing the close connection between town and countryside
20 Multiple defensive ditches

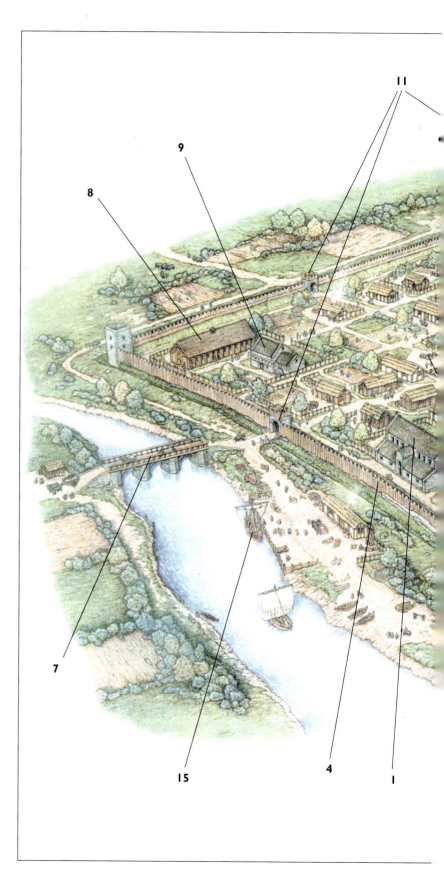

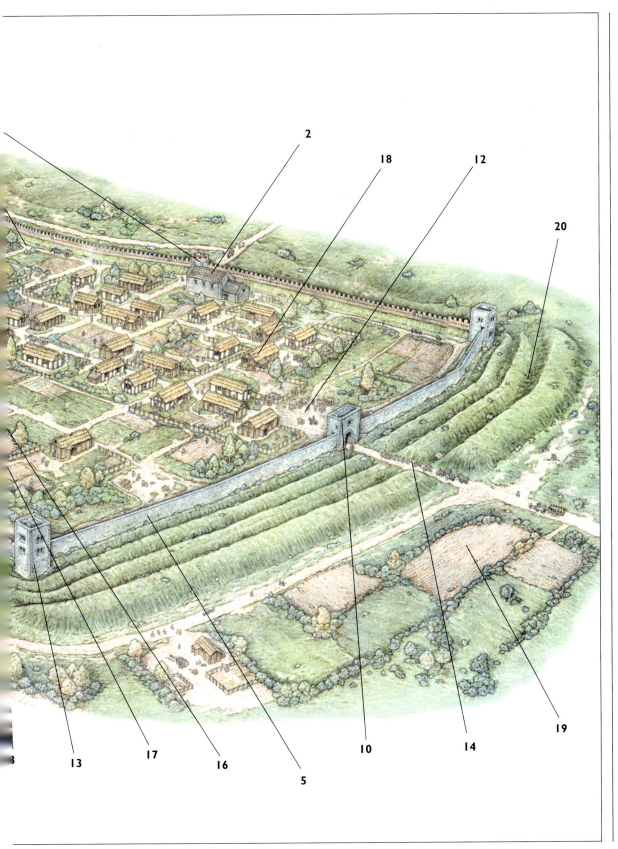

2

18

12

20

13

17

16

5

10

14

19

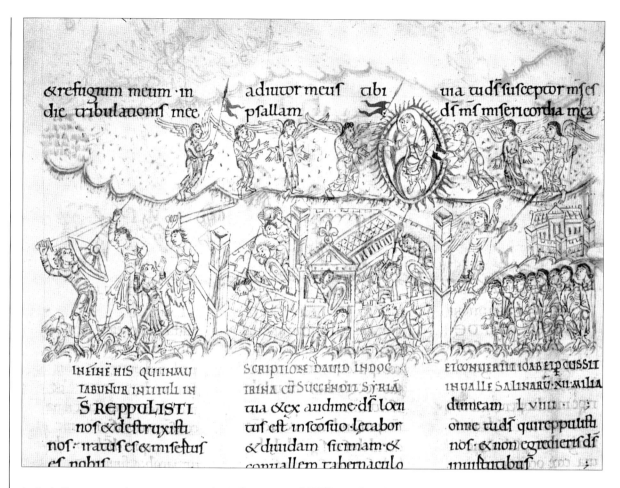

In line his quinam tabunur intiuli in ... s reppulisti nos & destruxisti nos; iratus es & misertus es nobis

scriptione dauid in doc trina cu succendit syria uia & ex audime df loci tui est in scosuo; letabor & diuidam sicimam & conuallem tabernaculo

et conuertit ioab et percussit in ualle salinaru; xii; milia dum eam; l; viii ... omne tudf quireppulisti nos; & non egredieris df in uirtutibus

An Anglo-Saxon manuscript illustration (British Library Harley MS 603, redrawn at Canterbury from an earlier Carolingian manuscript) showing an attack upon a city. The walled city here represents an Early Medieval view of a biblical city, but the siege itself represents a scene that may be understood (and feared) by its audience. The casting of stones from the ramparts shows that whereas arrows could be shot and javelins thrown at an attacking enemy from a safe distance, once the enemy actually got to the walls the situation became a great deal more desperate and the crude simplicity of a large stone dropped from a height took on a level of effectiveness. (By permission of the British Library, Harl. MS 603, fol. 32v)

against the army of William the Conqueror in 1066 and even Ealdorman Byrhtnoth's mustered force against the army of Olaf Trygvasson and Swein Forkbeard in 991, battle in the open field may have been preferred, although this may at least have been a concession to warrior pride.

If the leader in charge of the defence of a *burh* was to mount an effective defence he needed to keep forces in reserve ready to ensure that even if walls or gate were breached, an attacking army could not carry through the advantage, as defenders would be moved from one part of the fortification to another relatively quickly. To this end, internal lines of communication were important. Houses should only have been built some distance from the walls and a clear space should have been provided to get to the ramparts from the inside; internal roads should have been provided, some running diagonally, and everything possible done to slow down the enemy on his approach to the walls – whether by the use of multiple ditches, 'killing grounds' or even marshy ground upon one side of the settlement.

The sites

The designs of Anglo-Saxon burghal fortifications varied widely, but a common factor appears to have been a certain efficiency of construction. Under the programme instituted by King Alfred, the West Saxons utilised existing sites or at least the most suitable naturally defensible sites wherever possible.

In some cases, it was a relatively simply task to rebuild or modify Roman fortifications at places where the original walls survived but may have needed repairs. Examples of these are Roman towns such as Winchester (Hants.), Bath (Somerset), Exeter (Devon) and Chichester (Sussex) and the former Roman shore fort at Portchester (Hants.). Other Roman town walls survived in Dorchester (Dorset) and Canterbury (Kent), and it is surprising that no provision was made for their re-use in the *Burghal Hidage*. One possible explanation is that perhaps Dorset was sufficiently provided for in the late-9th century and did not need another fortification; the case of Kent is unusual and it is possible that this county had separate arrangements. Similarly, London, another important former Roman city, does not appear in the *Burghal Hidage*, although Southwark – on the opposite bank of the Thames – does, and there is some certainty that London was re-used as a fortified town during the reign of Alfred. This has been explained by the possibility that at the time that the surviving version of the *Burghal Hidage* was compiled, London was included under Mercian arrangements.

Such repair work upon Roman fortifications was probably undertaken in stone, as Anglo-Saxon builders constructed high-quality stonework, but in the conditions of the time, gaps in some of these walls may have been temporarily shored up with timber as formerly abandoned or under-populated Roman towns became important centres once more. However, these were not simply just recreations of Roman towns. At Winchester, archaeologists discovered that the Roman wall was not exclusively relied upon: a double ditch was excavated on one side of the city, and new gateways were probably constructed. Furthermore, the internal layout of the city was changed to incorporate defensive requirements including replacing the earlier Roman road system with a new grid-patterned system. It is difficult to discern the manner in which the walls were modified, but we can only assume that if walkways did not exist in the Roman stonework the West Saxons would have added these wherever possible, as there was no point in having a substantial walled fortification if there were no means by which the defenders could have seen any incoming forces.

In a few cases, most notably Wallingford (Berks., now Oxon.) and Cricklade (Wilts.), the West Saxons imitated the design of the Roman cities that they had inherited and constructed entirely new, large *burh*s. Even if the defences were more likely to have been made from wooden palisades than massive stone walls, the layouts of these *burh*s were impressively geometric and indicate a central authority with high pretensions. Excavations at Cricklade have also suggested the presence of at least one defensive tower on the ramparts and, as with other *burh*s constructed in a similar fashion, the defenders may have been able to move around the perimeter of the fortification using wooden walkways laid down upon the earthen ramparts. The site's triple ditches probably ensured that this *burh* presented an essential part of the defence of the northern frontier of the West Saxon kingdom.

There were also places where natural topography, such as the bend in a river or a promontory, allowed the construction of a highly defensible site. Examples of this are where a spur of high ground, such as at Shaftesbury or Malmesbury, provided what was effectively a 'new' hillfort. At Lydford, the route followed by

Winchester

The *burh* of Winchester and its surrounding landscape. As *Venta Belgarum*, Winchester had been a Roman provincial centre, which in turn had supplanted the Iron Age hillfort at St Catherine's Hill (to the south-east, at the bottom of the picture). West Saxon kings made use of the Roman city when they established the first bishop of Winchester at the Old Minster in the 7th century, but the refortification and regularised layout of the city, with its grid-pattern streets, was an achievement of the 9th century, arguably the work of King Alfred (871–99). Here, the city is shown at the beginning of the 10th century. As a well-fortified royal centre of the kingdom of Wessex, Winchester was well placed in the valley of the River Itchen at the convergence of four Roman roads, which allowed the rapid movement of armies across the kingdom. In the far distance, to the east of the city, a beacon fire has been lit. Such beacons provided a network that could warn quickly and efficiently of the movement of invading armies, allowing troops within fortifications to react appropriately.

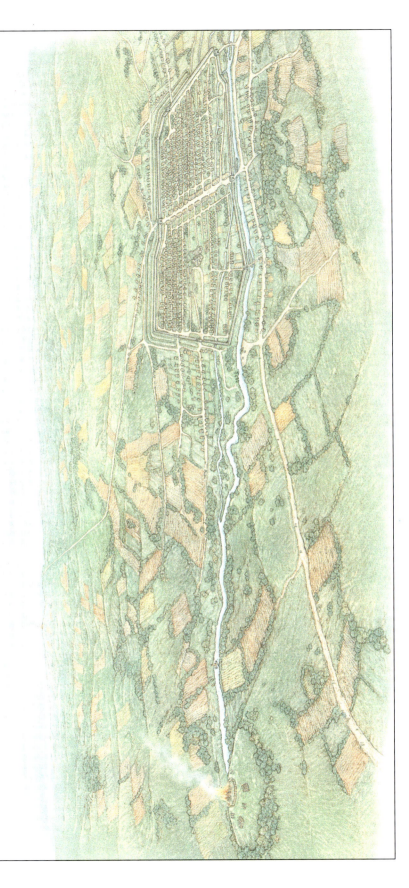

the river Lyd has created a deep natural gorge on three sides of the spur of land that became the town itself. This meant that the Lydford *burh* was nearly impregnable on these three sides, as the addition of small palisades or stone walls would have given a small number of defenders the cover they required to prevent an assault. The clearing of any vegetation and undergrowth, an important task at any site, would have been an especially onerous task here, but nonetheless essential as it would have prevented small groups of attackers from infiltrating the site.

The network of defence was completed by the addition of a number of smaller sites; these were generally hilltop sites, sometimes reused Iron Age hillforts. It is possible that such sites were not intended to remain operational in the long term, but may have been designed to serve as refuges for the population of the local area. Some were presumably garrisoned in some manner and did not rely solely upon the self-defence of the peasantry. It was such small fortresses, still maintained upon the principle of one hide of land, which may have been the biggest expenditure for the late-9th- and early-10th-century West Saxon state. Due to the trade that took place within them, fortified towns presumably paid for themselves, but in order for the system to be comprehensive, we may suspect that such smaller fortifications as the so-called 'emergency *burhs*' had to be subsidised. Considering the pressures involved in maintaining such fortifications they were probably the first to be disposed of in the 10th century, although similar fortifications needed to be resurrected later under the dangerous conditions of the reign of King Æthelred II.

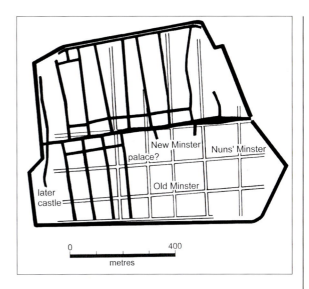

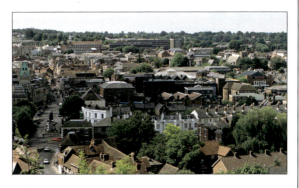

A plan of Winchester showing the change from the Roman to the 9th-century Anglo-Saxon street patterns (superimposed). This was a renewal of the Roman city on a level that showed a high degree of planning. The layout of the modern city, as may be discerned from the photograph taken from a hill at the east of the city, reflects this. (Redrawn after P. Addyman and D. Hill, 'Late Saxon Planned Towns', *Antiquaries Journal*, 51, 1971)

Existing defences, Roman, natural or otherwise, were simply a variation on a theme; the standard means of fortification in Wessex tended to be a ditch and a rampart, with some sort of structure, probably wooden, underlying the earthen rampart to give strength and prevent its collapse. This would often be crowned with a palisade, sometimes with towers to provide extra defence at weak points. Archaeological investigations have shown that the construction of these defences appears to have followed a generally standard design with some local variations (suggesting that there were different construction crews at work). This is not to suggest that a 'central' blueprint existed from which designs might follow. The local variations seem to have been the most logical manifestations of a centrally delegated task. For example, larger sites, such as Cricklade and Winchester often also necessitated the digging of multiple defensive ditches, presumably with the intention of disrupting an enemy attack before it had even reached the walls of the fortification.

The earth taken from the ditch would have been used in the construction of the ramparts. Their vertical external faces of the ramparts may have been strengthened to make them more difficult for attackers to surmount. While turf may have been added to hold the earthen ramparts together, it has been suggested that in some cases it was more effective to use palisades to create a continuous 10ft face for the defences.

In the later-10th century, there appears to have been an attempt to modify the defences across Wessex with the use of stone rather than timber to add strength to the fortifications. However, there is nothing in this to rival the achievement of the later-9th century, when such a large number of fortifications were organised and built in such a short time.

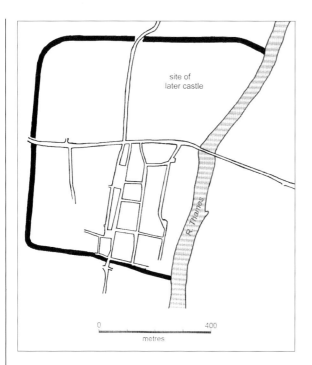

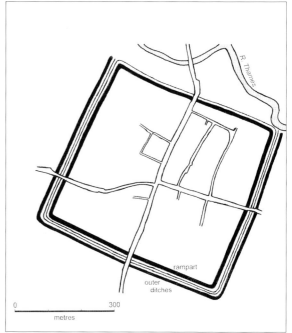

Wallingford (above left), formerly in Berkshire now in Oxfordshire, and Cricklade (above right and right), Wiltshire, 9th-century West Saxon 'planned towns', following patterns worthy of a Roman urban planner. The north-eastern burghal defences at Wallingford are only postulated here as this was the site of a later castle, but a full Anglo-Saxon defensive circuit is logical. Well-planned street patterns may have facilitated a more efficient defence in allowing troops to move around the ramparts. (Plans redrawn after J. Haslam (ed.), *Anglo-Saxon Towns in Southern England*, 1984; aerial photograph courtesy of Mick Aston)

(1) Lydford in Devon, (2) Shaftesbury in Dorset and (3) Malmesbury in Wiltshire; three places where the natural topography was incorporated into providing defences. At Shaftesbury and Malmesbury (see aerial photograph opposite, bottom left), this was in the form of the promontory of land upon which the fortifications were built, whereas in the case of Lydford (see photograph opposite, bottom right), a surrounding ravine was used as part of the defences. (Plans redrawn after Hill and Rumble, *Defence of Wessex*, and C. A. R. Radford, 'Later pre-Conquest Boroughs', *Medieval Archaeology*, 14, 1970)

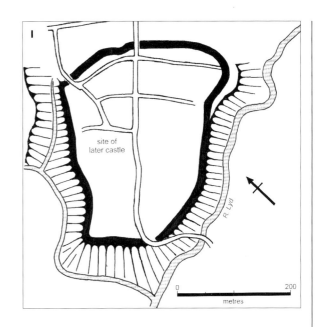

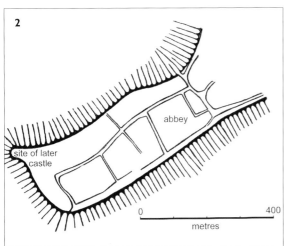

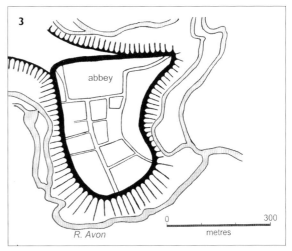

FOLLOWING PAGE **Lydford**

Standing on the edge of Dartmoor, Lydford was at the frontier of the West Saxon kingdom, at times trading with and at other times defending against the people of Cornwall nominally under West Saxon overlordship. As a frontier fortification, Lydford was also well placed to defend the supplies of silver mined in the south-west. The town was dramatically protected by the natural topography of a ravine on two sides. The ravine may now provide a pleasant backdrop to one of the more picturesque towns in South Devon, but in the Anglo-Saxon period it also meant that the fortification was virtually impregnable on two sides, a factor realised when the Normans later built a castle in the town. The West Saxons made good use of natural topography in their siting of fortifications, whether in the bend of a river, upon a natural promontory, but Lydford arguably provides the most dramatic example, as a force of Vikings discovered

in 997 when during a raiding expedition, which included the burning of the monastery at nearby Tavistock, they failed to capture the town. A benefit to the design of a such a naturally well-situated fortification may have meant that less resources were needed upon the less accessible sides in the form of men and materials. These could be concentrated upon the more vulnerable sides, as it would have taken some time for any attacking force to scale the sides of the gorge, during which more defenders could be brought to bear against them. The *Burghal Hidage* provides a notably low figure for Lydford, and a number of similarly placed *burhs*. There was a disadvantage to such policies, however, as the physical limits placed upon the town by such topography meant that it could be difficult for a town to extend beyond its natural boundaries. Partly as a result of this, like a number of the West Saxon fortifications, Lydford was to decline in the later Middle Ages.

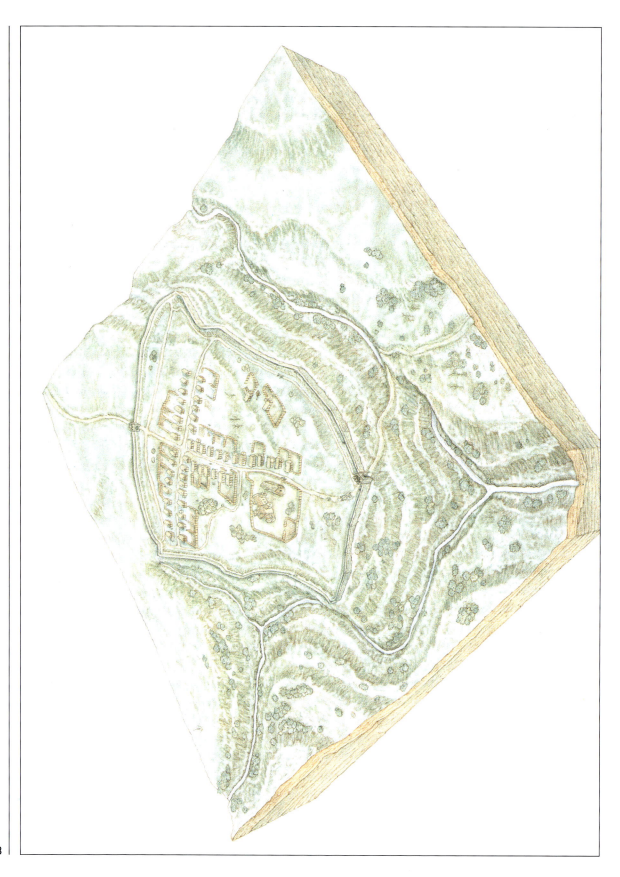

Town and garrison life

As has been seen, many of the larger *burhs* of Wessex became important as towns. Within the security of fortifications, urban economies could develop as *burhs* became centres for the buying and selling of the agricultural produce of the neighbouring region. The control of silver within them also meant that they could flourish as centres of the production of high quality goods such as leather and metalwork. In this respect, some historians have suggested that royal authority was the guiding power here, and the increase of royal authority may even have been the real intention that lay behind the construction of the *burhs* and the resultant control of the population and economy (even if, paradoxically, by the end of the Anglo-Saxon period, many of the larger towns had begun to develop a degree of civic independence). Of course, the Viking threat was no illusion, but it may have been in the interests of the king, specifically Alfred and his son Edward the Elder, to remind their subjects of the threat in order to ensure that the urban economy that developed under the first 'English' kings could be tightly controlled.

This meant that trade had to take place within the walls of the fortifications. Whether kings intended to stimulate trade in the kingdom by these means or simply ensure that they were able to gain a greater hold over the taxation of that trade remains a subject of debate; it is even possible that both were intended. However, during the course of the 10th century, the emergence and consolidation of the West Saxon Crown's control of the urban economy can be seen. This is demonstrated by the increasingly draconian laws that were promulgated during

In a few cases, as happened centuries earlier in the post-Roman period, Iron Age hillforts were re-employed as burghal fortifications. Such so-called 'emergency *burhs*' (the term is not a contemporary one) were not ideal sites for urban life, but they may have filled gaps in the defensive system and, as the view from Chisbury hillfort demonstrates, they dominated much of the surrounding landscape.

Although studies on the status of the Anglo-Saxon *ceorl* have shown that a person of a status less than that of the thegnly class could actually have considerable wealth, this should not underestimate the poverty of many in Anglo-Saxon society, including those of unfree status. It may have been such people who were pressed into service in large numbers in the construction and maintenance of the *burh*s. Here, the peasant is depicted in a rough tunic and breeches; the spade that he uses is made of wood, with only a metal tip. (Drawing by Don Lavelle)

the reigns of Athelstan (924–39), Edgar (957–75) and Æthelred II ('the Unready', 978–1016) decreeing the minting of coinage in urban sites and ensuring that trade was only allowed to take place within designated fortified sites.

Of course, this does not mean that we should underestimate the terror that the Vikings inspired in the English. Although Edward the Elder and his sons moved their area of operations northwards as they began to take control of the area of the 'Danelaw' and, even though there were no attacks on southern England by the Vikings for much of the 10th century, the fear remained a potent one. In the 950s, King Eadred bequeathed £1,600 into the care of his bishops for his subjects to be relieved from either a famine or the attacks of a 'heathen army if they need'. Though we have no record of such attacks in this period, the Vikings were still a real presence in Europe and it is little wonder that trading continued in the *burh*s. In one lawcode dating from around the late 920s, King Athelstan declared that 'every *burh* is to be repaired by a fortnight after Rogation days'. As Rogation Days were the three days preceding Ascension Day (which occurred 40 days after Easter Sunday), Athelstan's two-week deadline would have meant that *burh*s had to be ready for use by the time of the campaigning season of May or June. Even if this call to defend Wessex never came in Athelstan's reign (indeed many of the inhabitants of the town may have become negligent, allowing ditches to be filled with rubbish or neglecting the state of repair of the palisades), it showed that the king remained conscious of the fact that the fortifications may have been needed. Although military historians tend to neglect the study of southern English *burh*s between the reigns of Edward the Elder and Æthelred 'the Unready', when the attacks began again with renewed vigour, we need to be aware of the tensions between the ordinary urban lives of a civilian population (who nonetheless may have expected their kings to work miracles when a hostile army arrived) and the military requirements of the *burh*s.

During their normal working lives, many of the urban *burh*s seem to have functioned and flourished as markets and administrative centres. However, this may not have been the case for the 'emergency *burh*s', situated upon hilltops and perhaps too small to attract urban life. For the members of such unfortunate garrisons posted to live and work on these fortified sites, life may have been purely military in nature and rather less interesting than in the taverns of the larger sites. While urban life in late Anglo-Saxon England can hardly be compared to the thriving cultures of the likes of Later Medieval London or Paris, those posted to the smaller *burh*s had still drawn the short straw and it is little wonder that the continued existence of burghal sites relied upon the urban economy.

For the majority of peasants drafted in to work on the smaller fortifications, especially during the period of what may effectively have been 'emergency' arrangements under King Alfred, garrison life may also have been singularly dull. Although recent scholarship has gone some way towards readdressing the nobility and even professionalism of Anglo-Saxon thegns in warfare, it is easy to underestimate the importance of press-ganged peasantry in the building of Alfred's networks. For those living in areas such as around Winchester or London, the royal orders to work within the towns were probably not too onerous for a few months. However, an isolated hilltop *burh* would have been much less appealing. It has been suggested that it was conditions such as this that led to bored *ceorls* neglecting the fortifications of *Andredeswealde* (?Kent). As the *Anglo-Saxon Chronicle* recorded, this allowed the Vikings to take the *burh* with great ease in 892.

The proportions of able-bodied men designated for work within the fortifications suggests that many of the people had to make their living from the urban economy, and a fine line might be drawn between seeing the occupants as warriors or 'civilians'. If Alfred had expected as many as 27,000 men to be involved in the defence of the fortifications, the pressure on the cost of supplying these men may have been relieved by allowing the garrisons to earn something of a living within the towns into which they had been transplanted. At the very least, the forced creation of such a large number of 'new' communities must have provided an economic stimulus as new families grew up and tradesmen and craftsmen began to thrive in these areas. *Burhs* were hardly the bastions of male military cultures, but were working sites that developed lives of their own. This view is supported by the excavations of the populations of the Danish 'Trelleborg' fortresses, which had similar demographics to the West Saxon sites. Although the Danish fortresses were previously associated with the male warrior culture of the legendary Jomsvikings, archaeologists were surprised to find craft, industry and female burials. These were not simply camp followers, but are presumed to have been the wives of the warriors whose families lived and worked within the fortifications.

Archaeological excavations and later records of street patterns have tended to show that the larger towns, such as Winchester, tended to be 'zoned' with trades and crafts grouped into particular areas. This was hardly unique to the Anglo-Saxons and was a tendency that continued throughout the Middle Ages into the Early Modern period. Nevertheless, it is interesting to see the early development of such urban life within the city walls as, for example, Winchester's 'Fleshmonger Street', 'Parchment Street' and 'Tanner Street' became identifiable trading or craft-working areas during the Anglo-Saxon period.

From at least the early-10th century, coins were minted within towns, and such legislation as Athelstan's Grateley lawcode (so called by historians because it was declared at Grateley in northern Hampshire) show the attention given to this by kings. Athelstan made sure that the locations of the mints were known throughout his kingdom (north and south) and many were places described in the *Burghal Hidage*.

The making of the dies used to strike coins was skilled work, but the striking of the dies in order to make coins may have been a more simple process, as it involved the casting of 'blank' coins and the striking of one part of the die against the other in order to make the impression of the coin; modern reconstructions have shown that a mint could be set up, a sizeable batch of coins struck and be taken down within a few hours. However, as inertia has a tendency to develop around something technically 'mobile', mobility may have been more difficult in practice, especially as moneyers tended to be included amongst the richer members of urban society, presumably owning sizeable property within the towns.

Renewals of the coinage also appear to have taken place at intervals; coins had to be returned to a mint in order to receive the new issue of a particular type; old coins were (at least theoretically) illegal. This provided the moneyers and, through them, the king with a regular means of profit on the control of silver and may also have helped to prevent supplies of counterfeit coins from coming onto the market. Therefore, it was important for the mint to remain in a place where the local population knew it to be. As recipients of the wealth that was generated by the minting of coins, kings needed mints to remain in the same place as far as was possible. This, and the need to prevent the counterfeiting of coins, is reflected by the fact that a coin had the name of the moneyer who had struck it as well as the place where it had been minted.

Curiously, the importance of the mints is demonstrated by the very fact that at least two of them had to be moved in the early-11th century, when King Æthelred relocated them to more secure locations such as the Iron Age hillforts of South Cadbury (Somerset), Cissbury (Sussex) and Old Sarum (Wilts.), as the less well protected mints at Ilchester, Chichester and Wilton presumably received unwanted attention (Chichester is recorded in the *Burghal Hidage* and so was presumably fortified, but perhaps its 11th-century defences were not sufficient for a site so close to the coast). Such 'emergency *burhs*' may have been little more than a mint on a hilltop, but they still show the importance of the mint within the regional economies of Wessex.

Religious life

As well as providing a centre for the control of the economy and promotion of trade, many of the West Saxon *burhs* also contained religious centres in the form of mother churches often known as 'minsters'. While this is not the place for a discourse on the importance of the church in Anglo-Saxon life, important minster churches were often within the perimeter of the fortification and provided a focus for urban life and the local economy. Of course, with the role of the church as a production centre of Bibles and acquirer of precious artefacts this wealth may also have helped to attract Viking raiders, but that could hardly be helped. As an institution that was close to the royal family, whose members had, in many cases, founded the churches, the protection and defence of the church was a responsibility of the West Saxon king.

The view across northern Dorset afforded from the *burh* at Shaftesbury. Because of its position, Shaftesbury proved to be a strategic site for the defence of Wessex. Its natural promontory meant that it overlooked the Blackmore Vale and controlled all the nearby roads, but it is better remembered by contemporaries as a spiritual fortress. Founded as a nunnery for the daughter of King Alfred, around 888, it continued to have close connections with the West Saxon royal house.

An illustration of the proximity of Athelney (top left) and Lyng (foreground) in Somerset. Lyng was included in the *Burghal Hidage*, whereas Athelney was founded as a monastery, probably in commemoration of King Alfred's victory against the Vikings. A bridge was constructed to connect Athelney and Lyng across the marshy Somerset Levels (see p.29) and this photograph, taken during winter flooding, shows the importance of holding such dry high ground as Athelney and Lyng afforded. The second photograph (right) shows that the fortification at Lyng had to be limited to a small size along the high ground. (Photographs courtesy of Mick Aston)

The establishment of churches within newly founded *burh*s may reflect their central role in the urban life envisaged by West Saxon kings. In Shaftesbury (Dorset) and Athelney (Somerset) King Alfred founded monasteries with close connections to the West Saxon royal family on geographically defensible sites. In the case of Athelney, the royal monastery may even have become the primary function of the site, as the *burh* at Lyng appears to have taken over the defensive responsibilities for the area.

It may even be suggested that the church played an active role in the defence of the *burh*s in which they were situated. While there is little record of monks actually fighting against enemies in Anglo-Saxon England, pagan or otherwise, it is likely that churchmen had a part to play in financing the operations

A housecarl of the 11th century. Although sporting a round shield rather than a kite-shaped one, he is as well armoured as many of his European contemporaries. Such high-status warriors, with close connections to the royal family, may have held important positions in towns after the reign of Cnut, perhaps less for the defence of towns than to enforce the king's control of them. (Drawing by Don Lavelle)

of both defence and maintenance and may even have been responsible for the defence of stretches of wall (or in the case of Wimborne, for example, the whole site itself). At Portchester, Hampshire, it is possible that the monks of the Old Minster at Winchester, who had owned the land until the early-10th century, held this responsibility. This reflects the possibility that the dangers posed by the Vikings to the West Saxon kingdom were also an opportunity for the kings of Wessex to place tighter controls upon the money paid by the Church to the kingdom.

Religious festivals may have also lent a sense of theatre and drama to the developing West Saxon towns. On the day of the translation of St Swithun in Winchester, the monks of the Old Minster paraded the saint's bones from one church to another through the streets of the city. We can only imagine the colours, smells and sounds of such an event and the role that it played in the lives of the people in the town. It is worthwhile to at least appreciate the centrality of the belief in the protective powers of saints in popular religious belief; to the Anglo-Saxons of over a millennium ago, faced with attacks by those they considered to be violent pagans, this was an important aspect of defence.

Warrior elites: the housecarls

In the early-11th century, following his conquest of the English kingdom in 1016, King Cnut appears to have introduced a new form of 'professional' warrior closely tied to the royal house. The housecarls (*huscarle*) were the elite forces close to the king and royal family, ready to fight and die for them; they included those who fought on the slopes of Senlac Hill with Harold in 1066 and were those trusted by King Harthacnut to sack the town of Worcester in 1042 for non-payment of tax. After the Danish conquest of 1016 it was important to ensure that the king's men, those who newly owed allegiance to the king, such as the Godwine family (raised to prominence by King Cnut) were based within the increasingly independent towns. Although the differing ways in which Domesday Book records dues and customs in towns makes it notoriously difficult to make comparisons between counties, there are records of housecarls in towns in at least Dorset and Berkshire and it is entirely possible that other southern English towns had similar groups of quasi-professional troops. For example, the Domesday entries for Kent describe the king's right to the provision of a bodyguard for six days when he came to Sandwich or Canterbury.

The king and the towns

Kings may have had residences within the walls of urban fortifications, at least in times of potential trouble. In times of peace, kings were more likely to have spent time away from towns in hunting lodges and rural palaces such as that found at Cheddar in Somerset. Anglo-Saxon kings, like so many medieval rulers, did not remain in one place but moved from one residence to the next according to circumstances and the supplies of food and drink due to them. However, the protection of the supplies of food and drink gathered from royal estates had been an important factor behind the decision to construct the network of *burh*s in the first place. Whether or not the king came to the *burh*, harvest times must have been bustling centres of activity as any surplus food was sold off in the market places.

Some West Saxon kings may have taken the decision to build a residence a short distance from the town. For example, charters show that a royal residence may have been built some two miles outside Winchester at Kings Worthy in order to allow the king to make decisions free from the influence of the powerful Bishop of Winchester, while being close enough to be involved with urban life. The life within the town itself must have bustled during times when the king gathered the great and good of the kingdom around him for royal assemblies.

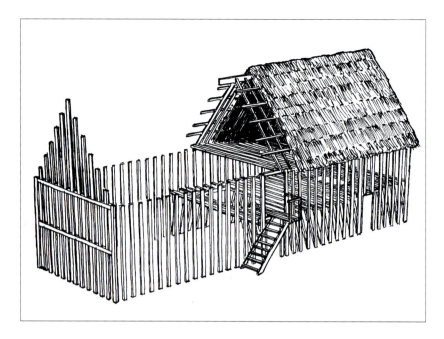

Reconstruction of a high-status hall of the 10th century, based upon that excavated at Cheddar (Somerset). The construction of a second storey meant that the position of the important magnates could be differentiated from those who served them. Noble or even royal halls such as this may also have been constructed in parts of West Saxon towns. (Drawing by Don Lavelle)

Image from an 11th-century manuscript depicting Christ as a warrior leading his troops to a walled town. The experience of siege was a common one for the inhabitants of Wessex and was an important part of Early Medieval warfare. (By permission of the British Library, Harl. MS 603 fol.13v)

However, in times of trouble, such as those faced by Alfred and Æthelred, such a policy was probably a luxury that the king could ill afford. Athelney in Somerset and Chippenham in Wiltshire were fortified places that provided a refuge for King Alfred in the 9th century. Æthelred used the increasingly important town of London as his base during the period of the invasion of the army of Swein Forkbeard. We should not overlook the fact that in times of peace, too, towns provided useful central sites for the gathering of assemblies.

Campaigns in Wessex and fortifications

Sieges in Early Medieval Wessex

No comprehensive description survives of the conduct of a siege in Anglo-Saxon England. Indeed, in terms of written sources very little survives that relates to sieges in any great detail, beside the occasional case of an army sitting outside a fortification. By comparison with the continental European experience, where the Vikings' infamous siege of Paris in 885/6 made a king of the Frankish defender Count Odo, the student of Anglo-Saxon England might be forgiven for assuming that siege warfare was uncommon before 1066.

There are cases of armies sitting outside fortifications, but these do not seem to have lasted long. The West Saxon army's wait outside the Viking refuge at Chippenham (Wilts.) into which Guthrum's army had retreated after the defeat at Edington may have been extraordinary for its long duration, especially as, according to Asser, King Alfred had seized all the men, cattle and horses he had found outside the fortification. However, there is little record of the atrocities meted out against the defeated army once they had finally capitulated as it was too important for Alfred to ensure that he could make a lasting peace with his Viking enemy; in effect, to baptise him and create him as a Christian king in his own image. While the Vikings may have been desperate, the 'rules' of siege warfare may not have developed to the extent which they were to develop in later centuries in which once the first stone had been thrown there would be no 'honourable surrender' but simply the slaughter of the besieged or (more likely) the starvation, infestation and retreat of the besiegers. By comparison, Alfred's peace with the defeated Vikings was certainly an honourable one.

It is the reign and activities of Alfred's son King Edward the Elder against the Viking and Mercian *burh*s of the Danelaw that showed that the Anglo-Saxons could actually have quite sophisticated notions of siege warfare, as Edward and his sister, Æthelflaed (the famous 'Lady of the Mercians') were often ready to build fortifications a short distance – for example, across the river – from an existing *burh* in order to outlast the enemy whom they were besieging (these were the origins of the so-called 'double *burh*s', one example of which may have been at Bedford). Such techniques compare well with the building of siege castles in later centuries and may have developed through Edward the Elder's use of Badbury Rings as a base in his siege of his cousin at Wimborne Minster (Dorset) in 899 or 900. Ultimately, however, such siege techniques as those used in Mercia against the Vikings were probably based on recognition of the fact that West Saxon armies had the luxury of operating close to home (or at least within reasonably easy reach), whereas in the hostile territory of the West Saxon kingdom, Viking armies relied upon constant movement in order to survive in enemy territory. Against an army whose strength was their own mobility, the burghal system of fortifications proved a major obstacle.

For all this, siege warfare does not seem to have developed to the extent that siege weapons were used in the taking of fortifications. Such machines of war were probably refined in Europe as a result of the Crusades, but they may well still have existed in Early Medieval Europe and may not have been completely unknown to the Anglo-Saxons. As their neighbours the Carolingian Franks had proved a great influence in so many aspects of English life, it would be difficult to believe that this did not also apply to siege warfare. One of Charlemagne's *capitularies*, the documents recording royal and imperial policy, records the arrangements of Frankish siege-trains. Later, in the 9th century, the monk Abbo tells us that at Paris in 885/6, the Vikings used battering rams and siege engines to throw missiles at the Franks. The Carolingian Franks had not been unprepared either, as they used a mixture of oil, wax and pitch as well as *ballistae* against their besiegers, and reinforced their fortifications with wooden structures. Of course, as ever with medieval accounts of warfare, we should not dismiss the possibility that Abbo may have been rather influenced by classical models of warfare in his portrayal of the siege of Paris, but neither should we ignore the fact that the scholars at the West Saxon court, so influential in the policies of King Alfred, were equally well versed in the writings of classical authors and the West Saxon court's official record, the *Anglo-Saxon Chronicle*, took a special interest in happenings across the Channel in the 880s.

The reasons why there is no record of a prolonged Viking siege of a West Saxon *burh* to compare with the Parisian example are probably political; in the 880s the Vikings controlled or had political influence over large amounts of territory in the region of the upper Seine in Francia; by comparison with Viking fortunes in Wessex, they had the time and the control of territory, as well as the lines of communication, to undertake such a siege. It is possible that only King Alfred's decisive act of summoning his entire army to fight the Vikings at Edington in 878 saved him from such a protracted siege against his fortress at Athelney, as it was arguably only in that year, when the Vikings had seized control of so much of the West Saxon kingdom, that the conditions would have been favourable to their prosecution of such a siege as later occurred at Paris.

However, *burhs* remained important factors in operations. Even in 876, before the *burh* system was in place, the Vikings attacked the nunnery at Wareham and then remained besieged in the town before they made their escape. Asser refers to it as a *castellum* (meaning 'fortified place' rather than 'castle'). This suggests that there were some substantial fortifications in place that could be used by the Vikings as defences, turning the resources of the West Saxon kingdom against itself. It has been suggested that Wareham may have had inherent weaknesses that allowed it to be taken over so quickly. Specifically, the area along the riverside may not have been fortified as no remains of a rampart have been found here and the *Burghal Hidage* arrangement equates almost perfectly with the length of the ramparts on the western, northern and eastern sides. If so, Wareham may have been arranged in this manner to allow river trade to arrive at the site, possibly relying upon the presence of a bridge to the south-east in order to prevent attacking fleets penetrating the town. However, the alternative theory, that the church and settlement were simply unable to stand up to the pace of the Viking attack seems a more plausible hypothesis than to assume inherent design flaws. If, as seems likely, in 876 the West Saxon kingdom was not properly organised for its defences in the manner in which it was to be in the 890s, then this may be enough to explain the success of the Viking fleet in the face of a fully constructed *burh*.

The enforced peace after the battle of Edington seems to have allowed King Alfred to reconstruct and fortify his kingdom. Although the *Anglo-Saxon Chronicle* makes little mention of the building campaigns that were required for the defence of the kingdom, they were still proceeding with a sense of urgency. It may well be the very absence of 'minor' Viking raids upon West Saxon towns or churches in the 880s that testifies to the success of the burghal system. The one Viking attack of this period, upon Rochester in Kent, was singularly unsuccessful. Richard Abels has referred to this period as one of an 'uneasy peace', in which Alfred managed to seize control of the increasingly important *burh* at London. Here, the only Viking activity was at least not enough to threaten the security of the entire kingdom, as had been the case in the 870s.

However, in 892, the Viking threat resurfaced once more as a 'new' and substantial Viking army arrived in southern England fresh from campaigns in the West Frankish kingdom. This force attacked an unfinished *burh* in the

Andredeswealde, probably in the Weald of Kent somewhere near the River Lympne, a place sometimes thought to have been the unidentified *burh* of *Eorpburnan*. This was a wake-up call to a kingdom that had made a successful peace with one group of Vikings. However, the fact that the Viking army had to attack an unfinished *burh* suggests that they were experienced from problems in Francia, including the failure to seize Paris in 886.

The Viking army had presumably learnt that attacks on fortifications were not to be undertaken lightly and this may explain why an unfinished *burh* with an under-strength and poorly motivated garrison of *ceorls* was the target. These few bored peasants pressed into labour on the fortification may have yielded little in the form of stolen booty, but in the late-9th century Vikings intended to seize more than this. There were political aims at stake and the defeat of the West Saxon kingdom in open warfare may have become a tempting prize once more. As Simon Keynes has suggested, despite historians' concentrations on the crisis of the 870s, the Anglo-Saxon Chronicler's language has indicated that the threats of the 890s were just as serious. The Vikings' act of destroying a fortification and spreading a message of fear amongst the less motivated majority of their garrisons may have been an effective long-term objective. The fortress in the *Andredeswealde* may also have been an Achilles heel in the burghal system of Wessex, as it allowed the Vikings a foothold in the kingdom's south-eastern corner where two large Viking forces could rendezvous relatively protected from West Saxon retribution by the geography of the large Wealden forests.

However, this geography also had its disadvantages as it meant that for any gains to be successful the Vikings would have had to emerge into the web of West Saxon fortifications in Wessex itself. If the Vikings had intended to undertake a sustained campaign against the fortifications of Wessex in the 890s they were not successful and had to content themselves with attacking the peripheries of the kingdom. There was to be no equivalent of the audacious surprise attack on Chippenham in the West Saxon heartland of Wiltshire as had happened in 878. The places that could be attacked were those that could be reached by sea or river estuary, such as the area to the north of London where the Vikings contented themselves with building their own fortifications on the Thames rather than attempting to attack any of the *burh*s. The only West Saxon *burh* to be besieged was Exeter on the southern coast of Devon,

Wareham, Dorset, a site that may have been fortified before King Alfred's victory in 878. However, its waterfront along the river Frome may not have been fortified, a factor that may have led to its vulnerability against the Vikings in 876.

Assault on a burh

The attackers' view of an assault upon a West Saxon burh. Vikings attempt to charge up the outer ditch while a motley crew of Anglo-Saxon defenders demonstrate the manner in which a fortification could act as a force multiplier. Although there are some continental accounts of the use of siege engines around the 9th and 10th centuries these may have been influenced by classical accounts of warfare and here a somewhat more dangerous, although logistically simpler, direct assault is attempted. The Burghal Hidage, an early 10th-century document, notes that a pole of wall (5½ yards) could be defended by four men. One man entrusted with the defence of just over 3ft of wall may have resulted in rather crowded ramparts under normal circumstances (although we should still bear in mind that these were similar distances to the so-called 'shield-wall' formation), and in practice may have been unwieldy, but the flexibility in deploying troops inside the fortification may have allowed the defenders to bring more troops to bear where the attackers were in danger of breaching the defences. Although warfare in the Early Medieval world was often the preserve of the well-armed nobility, in such desperate circumstances poorly armed townsmen and local peasants might be brought into the defence of a fortification, and from the height of the ramparts a lucky throw of a spear or even a rock by such a defender could bring down even the fiercest of Viking attackers.

a fortification that managed to hold off the besieging Viking army until Alfred arrived with 'all the English Army' to relieve the town. Although the Viking force escaped, the repaired Roman walls of the *burh* managed to prevent Exeter's seizure. Much the same thing happened at Chichester in the last decade of Alfred's reign, when the Vikings ravaged parts of Sussex but were met by the townspeople (*burhware*), who, according to the *Anglo-Saxon Chronicle*, put the Vikings 'to flight and killed many hundreds of them and captured some of their ships'. Although we should allow for the probable exaggeration of the *Chronicle*'s language, this may well have been a ringing endorsement of Alfred's policy of retaining specialised garrison troops. The effectiveness of the *burhs* may not have lain solely in the fact that they could be formidable obstacles but also in the fact that their garrisons could make an unexpected sortie against an attacking force. Perhaps it was largely due to the defensive network that the Vikings did not dare to venture far inland.

West Saxon *burhs* seem to have remained unscathed for the rest of King Alfred's reign. It was in the months following the death of King Alfred in October 899 that a member of the West Saxon royal house, Æthelwold, seized the town of Wimborne Minster in Dorset, declaring his intention to, according to the *Anglo-Saxon Chronicle*, 'live there or die there'. He had also seized the strategically situated *burh* at *Twynham* (Christchurch) on the coast, perhaps to ensure that he had a safe route by which he could make his escape.

However, the actions of the renegade Æthelwold continue to puzzle. If the *burh*s of Wessex had stood up so well against large Viking armies, why did they collapse so quickly in the face of this rebel member of the royal family? The answer may lie in the fact that Æthelwold was indeed a member of the royal family in the time of confusion following the death of such an influential king as Alfred. Indeed, if Æthelwold arrived as a claimant to the throne, the people of the western part of Wessex may have believed that there was little reason to bar the gates against him.

Badbury Rings, Dorset, site of a temporary camp made by the young King Edward the Elder against his rebellious brother, Æthelwold, who had attempted to seize power in western Wessex after the death of King Alfred in 899. The use of fortifications in siege warfare became an important factor in the strategies employed by King Edward.

South Cadbury, Somerset. This western British hillfort (see p.9) was used during the reign of King Æthelred II in order to protect one of the regional sites where coins were minted. High-quality faced stonework was used in the construction of the early-11th-century fortification. (Illustration by Don Lavelle)

In the face of the siege by King Edward the Elder, like any good Viking force (Æthelwold was later to lead a force of Vikings against his cousin in East Anglia), Æthelwold and his men made good their escape under the cover of darkness. If the West Saxons had used the element of surprise to good effect with their *chevauchée* from Chichester in 894, Edward was denied his prize by the use of a similar tactic.

There were few disturbances to the burghal system in Wessex for much of the 10th century, as West Saxon kings concentrated upon seizing and consolidating power in the midlands and north of England, even, under King Athelstan (924–39), heading north into what is now Scotland. Newly constructed *burh*s were used as bases for the gradual conquest of territory. Arguments can be made for suggesting that the systems of administration, including a system of burghal defence, were the import of a West Saxon system to the extent that England became a larger version of Wessex.

The period that saw the reprise of the burghal system in the defence of the southern part of the kingdom was the reign of Æthelred II ('the Unready', 978–1016). Although his reign ended ingloriously with illness and the division of the kingdom, for much of the period the burghal system was used to great effect against invading Viking armies. It may well have been the administration of this system that prevented the kingdom from collapsing earlier and arguments have been made that many of the large taxes known as 'Danegeld' levied by the West Saxon kingdom were used on defensive measures as well as to pay Viking armies to go away.

*Burh*s were often the targets for Viking attackers in the reign of Æthelred II; the first Viking attacks of his reign included raids on Southampton, which

The hillfort at Old Sarum, near the later town of Salisbury, Wiltshire, was also used during Æthelred's reign as a late 'emergency *burh*'. Used after the Norman Conquest as the site of a royal castle and cathedral church, Old Sarum was a well-defended site with a complex of deep ditches. (Aerial photograph courtesy of Mick Aston)

resulted in a Viking victory, and Watchet in Somerset, which was an early success for the Anglo-Saxon defenders. The relative success of the Viking armies may suggest that the burghal system in Wessex had been relatively neglected during the 10th century, and it may have been with a sense of alarm that some of the fortifications were revived. It is possible that the primarily military functions of the 9th- and early-10th-century *burh*s had been subsumed beneath the urban functions of what in many cases had become towns. However, that is not to underrate the effectiveness of the fortifications, some of which were repaired, renewed and rebuilt during the 10th century, even if the specialist *burhware* were no longer present. Even if thegns were still present in the towns, they did not provide an effective defence. The attackers faced by the English kingdom of Æthelred II were, after all, professional Viking raiders often fighting in large armies under Danish royal sponsorship.

However, in some cases, the *burh*s remained effective. Moving briefly outside Wessex, the defences presented by the *burh* of Maldon in Essex meant that an attacking Viking army had to remain on Northey Island. Although the results of the battle are well known as the Viking army managed to defeat the English force of Ealdorman Byrthtnoth in the battle celebrated in the Old English poem, the *burh* of Maldon escaped relatively unscathed.

In 1006 a Viking army that had been operating along the river Thames and, having defeated an English force sent out to fight them, marched south along a Roman road to their ships on the south coast. In the *burh* of Winchester the citizens breathed a sigh of relief as the army passed by the gates; the *Anglo-Saxon Chronicle* implies that the citizens had had a lucky escape. However, in view of the size of the Winchester *burh* this was not luck but the fact that the Viking army would have been unable to capture or sack the town without great difficulty, especially as they were effectively trying to make good their getaway.

This was the point of the *burh*s; in defensive terms it was far better for them to work as deterrents, with the larger defences tending to be more effective. Even when attacking smaller *burh*s, the Vikings were rarely successful in direct assaults but relied more on drawing English forces out into wild goose chases. In the cases of Southampton and Exeter, larger *burh*s, the coastal or estuarine nature of their locations helped ensure their capture. In the case of Exeter, the Anglo-Saxon Chronicler blamed a queen's French reeve (officer) by the name of Hugh for his treachery in 1003, and similarly the treachery of a certain archdeacon is blamed for the cause of the fall of Canterbury and the subsequent capture of its archbishop in 1011. If these 'traitors' were more than scapegoats, perhaps the Vikings needed to rely upon intrigue to be let into the town rather than via solely laying siege.

Defending the walls

Due to the lack of written sources, the ways in which an Anglo-Saxon *burh* was defended must remain largely conjectural. However, we can logically assume that missile weapons, light throwing spears and bows all played an important part in the defence of the *burh*s. As written sources rarely mention the use of missile weapons (apart from in the *Battle of Maldon* poem, where the language is ambiguous, many of the missiles used may either have been javelins, arrows, or even ordinary spears), military historians have tended to assume that the Anglo-Saxons had disproportionately small numbers of archers amongst their ranks. Given the need to shoot attackers before they could reach the walls or gates of the *burh* and the 'killing zone' provided by ditches, double ditches or even triple ditches, the use of bows seems perfectly logical in defending the walls. Although crossbows may have been known in later Anglo-Saxon England (much has been made of a stone carving of an Early Medieval Pictish archer and William of Poitiers' description of *ballistae* at the Battle of Hastings), there is little direct evidence to suggest that the crossbow was a weapon of Anglo-Saxon warfare, well suited though it proved to be for 12th- and 13th-century siege warfare.

In the final analysis, we must accept the limitations of the evidence. However, we know that the network of *burh*s was designed to present a network of formidable obstacles; the nature of this network seems to have meant that an invading force often had no option but to attempt to seize these fortifications. In some cases, the attackers succeeded by means fair or foul, but in others the fact that they did not succeed ensured the survival of the West Saxon kingdom.

An archer draws his bow against a target at a low trajectory. While because it seems that the Anglo-Saxons used fewer archers than their Norman adversaries in 1066 it is often assumed that Anglo-Saxon armies generally used few archers, the use of bows in the defence of ramparts seems highly probable, as they gave a potentially long defensive range in comparison to the 'medium' range of javelins. (Drawing by Don Lavelle)

Aftermath

In the 10th century, the smaller *burh*s – the likes of Sashes, Burpham and Chisbury – seem to have fallen out of use once more, and it has been suggested that this was because there were fewer economic reasons for them to continue to be maintained and garrisoned. On the other hand, however, those *burh*s that seem to have been intended as 'planned towns' went from strength to strength, the most obvious example of an increasingly successful urban economy based upon its geography and town design being that of London. Even if it would be going too far to suggest that the economy of the West Saxon kingdom and, later, English kingdom was founded by the building of *burh*s, their construction did at least prove an important factor in its promotion.

While the heyday of Alfred's system of defences was during the reign of Alfred himself and that of his son Edward the Elder, West Saxon defences were put to little military use for much of the 10th century. Viking attacks during the later 10th century may have brought the system under sharp focus once more, but it was as towns and the centres of economic and administrative power that *burh*s were now attacked. In the 11th century, William the Conqueror was to discover the political power wielded by the *burh*s of the Anglo-Saxons as Exeter attempted to provoke rebellion, their argument being that the new king was undermining the semi-independence of the towns in the English regions.

King William managed to bring the citizens of Exeter to agreement, but he had learnt a hard lesson. Medieval English kings denied the rights of townsfolk at their peril. A fortified wall was to become the distinguishing feature of the so-called 'borough rights' so cherished by Later Medieval towns (the term 'borough', indeed, came from the Old English word *burh*), but this was not simply a question of symbolism. A fortified wall gave a town a degree of independence from royal authority, a right to levy its own taxes and decide its own civic administration.

Although a good number of the *burh*s seems to have survived to 1066, and Domesday Book's records of the rights attributed to the different sites can generally be relied upon, during the decades beyond the Norman Conquest the *burh*s ceased to be the key system that could be called upon for the defence of the kingdom. Arguably this may have been the case from the conquest of Æthelred II's kingdom in 1016, but the Norman Conquest dramatically highlighted the change. Viking raiders could still present a threat in the 11th century and had attacked Sandwich in 1047, but after 1066 they limited their activities to the north. In any case, the private warfare of William the Conqueror's barons meant that the community-focused *burh*s were supplanted by a network of privately owned castles – royal, baronial and knightly – which formed the system of control of the kingdom's central points. While private fortifications were known in later Anglo-Saxon England, the Norman Conquest first saw the widespread use of the castle as a military weapon and administrative tool, in some places ensuring that rather than adding to the defence of a town, the town itself would be dominated by the brooding presence of a castle.

The fortifications of towns still had their part to play in the warfare of the following centuries, however, even if the specialised siege machinery designed for castles made short work of the stone walls of a fortified town. This was especially the case during the civil war fought between King Stephen and the Empress Matilda from 1139 to 1148. The war reached its height in the summer of 1141, when a 'double siege' was undertaken of the city of Winchester; the Empress Matilda held the city in order to besiege the Bishop of Winchester within Wolvesey Castle in the south-east of the city, while the king's men besieged the city itself. The desperate measure of burning the city undertaken by the Bishop's men shows the city's importance, even if such an action could not put a decisive end to either the siege or the war.

In the English Civil War of the 17th century, Anglo-Saxon fortifications were put into action, as garrison towns became the primary means of controlling territory. The fortifications developed by Alfred the Great were hardly the only means of providing defence, but in an age of gunpowder and large armies, in which the castle was no longer a primary means of defence, the fortified town became an important factor once more.

Three centuries later, in the summer of 1940, the fortifications of the former West Saxon kingdom were pressed into use for an invasion that was met with as much sense of dread as any Viking onslaught. Once more, towns had become the potential targets, something to defend rather than a means of providing defence. Bunkers and concrete pillboxes were the castles of the day, but it is an interesting footnote to an illustrious history that in one example, the walls of the *burh* of Wareham were expected to stand against German tanks and were especially refortified for the purpose. Like many citizens of the West Saxon kingdom a millennium earlier who gave thanks that they had survived another year without suffering the ravages of the Northmen, the citizens of this small Dorset town must have been equally pleased when autumn passed into the winter of 1940/41, and the fortifications of the town never had to be put to the test.

Anglo-Saxon fortifications were often incorporated into the defences presented by post-Conquest castles. Portchester, in Hampshire, shows the historical continuity of a single site, from Roman fortress to Anglo-Saxon *burh*. In the 12th century a square keep was added that made use of the Roman defences as a curtain wall.

Visiting Alfred's Wessex

The Early Medieval line of defences at Wareham was intended to hold back the projected German invasion of Operation Sealion in 1940. A pillbox was emplaced along the northern wall, on the entrance to the high street, and the western rampart was rebuilt in order to provide a strong anti-tank defence. Aptly, the level to which this was rebuilt may have been similar to that of the Early Medieval defences.

Many of the fortified towns of the *Burghal Hidage* still survive today in the form of small market towns of the type so beloved in the promotion campaigns for British tourism. These are, of course, a world away from the violence and, in many cases, the bustle of rural markets of a millennium ago. While none of the Anglo-Saxon palisades and little of the stonework are now visible, armed with a little imagination it is often possible to get a sense of the depths of history, the important battles, major strategic decisions and perhaps more importantly the lives of the ordinary men and women who populated the embryonic towns of Alfred's Wessex. Fortunately, it is still possible to trace the lines of ramparts around the perimeters of a number of sites and see where the layouts of streets allowed means of access across the fortifications. Even where the Roman and Anglo-Saxon walls have effectively been replaced by Later Medieval works, at Winchester (where walls survive around the cathedral close) and Chichester (Sussex) it is still worth seeing the integrity of a fortified medieval town. A similar argument could be applied to Southampton, where the medieval walls survive to a surprising extent in what is more usually considered to have been a city wholly and unsympathetically rebuilt after the bombing of World War II (there is some argument as to whether the modern city itself or the smaller suburb of Bitterne is the descendant of the Anglo-Saxon *burh* – although the argument for the latter is not a strong one). However, where earthworks stand in the forms of ditches and ramparts in such less heavily populated towns as Wareham (Dorset), Cricklade (Wilts.) and Wallingford (Oxon.), the sight is impressive. Ramparts may have become gentler over the centuries; ditches shallower and sometimes overgrown with brambles, but the sense of discovery that this allows the interested visitor can be quite overwhelming.

Of the *burh*s with surviving earthen ramparts, Wareham in Dorset is worthy of a visit as this has an almost complete circuit of defences and the visitor is able to walk much of three of the four sides of the town. Beginning at the impressively high western walls of the town (those reinforced to provide some defence against German tanks) allows the visitor to comprehend the sheer size of the defences and, equally importantly, a tour of the ramparts in a clockwise direction allows the visitor to finish the tour by relaxing in the sun with liquid refreshment along the quayside of the river Frome, something that can add a particularly pleasant dimension to the consideration of Alfred's Wessex.

Furthermore, Wareham's 11th-century church of St Martin on the walls of the town adds to the manner in which the Anglo-Saxon past is woven into the life of the town, although sadly there is little of Anglo-Saxon Wessex to be seen in the town's museum. However, Corfe Castle is a short distance away along the A351; a picturesque castle ruin that dominates the landscape of the 'Isle' of Purbeck. Corfe Castle has more of a pre-Conquest past than the proprietors of the Castle, the National Trust, are ready to admit. This was the site of the murder of King Edward 'the Martyr' (975–78), and was an important Anglo-Saxon hunting hall – some archaeologists have gone as far as to suggest that the 'herringbone' pattern of the stonework in the earliest part of the castle may date from some years before the reign of William the Conqueror.

Wareham is particularly well served with direct railway access to and from London Waterloo (journey time 2 to 2.5 hours), but for much other travel in the area, the use of a car can be indispensable as rural bus services are few and far between (information can be gained through the Wareham tourist office, 01929 552740).

East Dorset also contains Wimborne Minster and the impressive multivallate Iron Age hillfort of Badbury Rings. Although there is little of the Anglo-Saxon past left in Wimborne beside antiquarian monuments, the hillfort is an example of how an earlier generation of fortifications could be pressed into service; the ramparts have a commanding view of former Roman roads and it is possible to see some distance across Dorset to the coast. The visitor can easily understand Edward the Elder's reasons for encamping his army here.

Any tour through Dorset could also include a visit to the picturesque hilltop town of Shaftesbury, a place that is reasonably well connected by road, at least by the standards of one of the last English counties without a motorway. Although there is little of the *burh* left to see, Shaftesbury's high location provides the visitor with the sense that the town may have been almost unassailable and the view provided over the Blackmore Vale is breathtaking.

Further north across the county border in Wiltshire, the cathedral city of Salisbury is worth visiting because of the manner in which the Iron Age hillfort known as Old Sarum was pressed into service as a burghal mint in order to replace neighbouring Wilton. Old Sarum is not actually in Salisbury itself, but rather some miles to the north of the city. The many different phases of occupation (Iron Age, Roman, Anglo-Saxon, and perhaps most famously the site of a Norman castle and now demolished cathedral), combined with its desolate windswept nature mean that it can be an evocative place for the visitor, despite the fact that the car park is within the walls of the fortification.

In Oxfordshire, modern administrative changes have meant that the county now contains two former *burh*s where previously there had only been one. The county town of Oxford is a bustling city, but with care the layout of the Anglo-Saxon defences can be followed in the pattern of the streets even if the Norman castle is really the earliest substantial monument. Wallingford, some 20 miles to the south, provides an interesting example of a small town with impressive surviving earthworks that can be followed. Sadly, there is little else to be seen but, like Wareham, it is worth perambulating the walls of the town.

In places in Wessex, the iconography of Anglo-Saxon England has been used for a number of purposes; at Shaftesbury, Anglo-Saxon artistic motifs were used in the design of the town's war memorial in a style perhaps fitting for its Early Medieval legacy.

In terms of 'emergency *burh*s', a rewarding example that is somewhat less touched by the modern world than Old Sarum is South Cadbury in south Somerset. Though only a short distance from the A303, this fast road does not intrude much on the atmosphere of the hillfort. The site has many associations with King Arthur, but South Cadbury should not be overlooked as a late Anglo-Saxon fortification. The layout of the hillfort survives remarkably well and in some places the surviving Æthelredian stone walls can be seen through the turf.

Despite the fact that it was an important town in the later Middle Ages Lydford, now a small village in rural Devon on the edge of Dartmoor, arguably has the distinction of being the quietest of the 'major' *burh*s. Therefore one is free to wander around without even the distractions of the modern English small town. The layout of the streets is reasonably visible in the village roads, and the ramparts can be made out quite easily in the fields. Lydford gorge, following the course of the river Lyd, is a place of beauty now owned and run by the National Trust and the survival of a Norman keep and castle mound add to the range of sites worth seeing. Lydford can be reached from the larger towns of Okehampton and Tavistock (the latter interesting as the site of an Anglo-Saxon minster church, attacked by the same group of Vikings who attempted to storm Lydford in 997).

At the other end of the urban spectrum is London; though hardly renowned for its Anglo-Saxon past, the square mile of the city itself can be worth a visit, especially on a weekend when much of the city can be virtually deserted and a lack of traffic makes it a little easier to conceptualise the city's Anglo-Saxon past. Fragments of Roman Wall (used by the Anglo-Saxons in providing the defences of the city) survive in places, the most impressive being at the site of the Museum of London, a place that is worth a visit for its Anglo-Saxon artefacts.

The visitor to Winchester may feel a little less hurried than in London and although Winchester can be easily reached on a day trip from the capital city (one hour on a direct by train from Waterloo) or from elsewhere via the M3 motorway or A34 roads, it is nonetheless worth spending more than a day in the city. The city's Westgate provides an idea of the importance of a gateway to the defence of the town, even if, as noted earlier, this is a Later Medieval defence rather than Anglo-Saxon. For the most part (ironically with the exception of the County Council's offices built during the 1960s) the architecture is sympathetic and, in viewing the layout of the city from St Giles's hill to the east of the city, it is a relatively simple task to comprehend the descent of the city from its medieval predecessors. Most importantly, however, the presence of the cathedral gives a very real sense of the importance of the church to the city; the cathedral close, consisting of the cathedral and its associated buildings (including a 12th-century bishop's palace, site of the siege of 1141), still take up a sizeable quarter of the intra-mural area of the city. The City Museum is also an important place for the Anglo-Saxon student to visit. Though small, it has some interesting finds from the important Winchester City excavations and some useful models showing the Roman and medieval development of the city.

Elsewhere in Hampshire, to the west of the large city of Portsmouth and in a small town incongruously tucked into an industrial belt, Portchester is an impressive surviving Roman shore fort with both Anglo-Saxon and Norman additions. The 12th-century stone keep dominates the site and its trustees, English Heritage, provide a useful exhibition that includes a consideration of Portchester's Anglo-Saxon past. Although it is not possible to walk the stone ramparts of the Roman fortress, the castle does at least provide an excellent view of the fortification as a whole as well as a view over the natural harbour that it commanded. The village of Portchester can be reached by train on the main Southampton to Portsmouth line, and from there it is a short and pleasant walk to the fortification.

With some 32 known sites named in the *Burghal Hidage*, not to mention other fortifications pressed into service by the West Saxon kings, it is hardly surprising that not all of these can be covered comprehensively here, and an attempt has been made (with the exceptions of London and Oxford) to limit the discussion to the 'historic' kingdom of Wessex to the south of the Thames Valley. However, as the visitor to Alfred's Wessex may discover, this is something of an artificial limitation, and in the small market towns of southern England there is a lot more to discover than just these examples given here. An understanding of the past is a personal matter, and each visitor will find places that capture their own imagination in different ways. When visiting sites in the former West Saxon kingdom it can be useful to observe places in relation to each other, between the town and the wider landscape in which it stood in the Anglo-Saxon period, considering also the rivers and the smaller settlements. Such a technique is a useful way of gaining a sense of the achievements of the West Saxon kingdom.

Further reading

Since the 1960s, the understanding of the *Burghal Hidage* and the administration of fortifications in Wessex has flourished partly as a result of urban archaeology and partly as a result of seminal work by Nicholas Brooks. A great deal of scholarship has been undertaken on the significance of urban and other defensive in the light of the *Burghal Hidage* document. The most comprehensive study of recent years remains that edited by David Hill and Alexander Rumble, who provide a useful gazetteer of the sites named in the *Burghal Hidage*. Works on Offa's Dyke are included here as they provide some sense of the development of fortifications, and some general works on specific fortifications are also included, along with details of works on Anglo-Saxon kings under whom West Saxon campaigns included the use of fortifications.

Abels, R. P., 'English Logistics and Military Administration, 871–1066: The Impact of the Viking Wars', in *Military Aspects of Scandinavian Society in a European Perspective*, AD 1–1300, ed. A.N. Jørgensen and B.L. Clausen (Copenhagen, National Museum of Denmark, 1997), pp.257–65

Abels, R. P., *Alfred the Great: War, Kingship and Culture in Anglo-Saxon England*, (Longman, 1998)

Brooks, N. P., 'The Unidentified Forts of the Burghal Hidage' *Medieval Archaeology*, 8 (1964), pp.74–89

Brooks, N. P., 'The Development of Military Obligations in Eighth- and Ninth-Century England' in *England before the Norman Conquest: Essays presented to Dorothy Whitelock*, ed. P. Clemoes and K. Hughes (Cambridge University Press, 1971), pp.69–84

Brooks, N. P., 'England in the Ninth Century: The Crucible of Defeat', *Transactions of the Royal Historical Society*, 5th series 29 (1979), pp.1–20

Fox, C., *Offa's Dyke: A Field Survey of the Western Frontier-Works of Mercia in the Seventh and Eighth Centuries A.D.* (London: British Academy, 1955)

Haslam, J. (ed.), *Anglo-Saxon Towns in Southern England* (Chichester: Phillimore, 1984)

Hill, D. H. (ed.), *Ethelred the Unready: Papers from the Millenary Conference* (Oxford: British Archaeological Reports, 1978)

Hill, D. H. and Rumble, A. R. (eds), *The Defence of Wessex: The Burghal Hidage and Anglo-Saxon Fortifications* (Manchester University Press, 1996)

Hill, D. H., and Worthington, M., *Offa's Dyke* (Stroud: Tempus, 2003)

Lavelle, R., *Aethelred II: King of the English, 978–1016* (Stroud: Tempus, 2002)

Noble, F., *Offa's Dyke Reviewed*, ed. M. Gelling (Oxford: British Archaeological Reports, 1983)

Ralegh Radford, C. A., *The Pre-Conquest Boroughs of England, Ninth to Eleventh Centuries* (London: British Academy [pamphlet], 1980)

Reuter, T. (ed.), *Alfred the Great: Papers from the Eleventh-Century Conference* (Aldershot: Ashgate, 2003)

Reynolds, A.J., *Later Anglo-Saxon England: Life and Landscape* (Stroud: Tempus, 1999)

Williams, A., 'A Bell-House and a Burhgeat: Lordly Residences in England before the Norman Conquest', *Medieval Knighthood* 4 (1992) pp.221–40

Yorke, B., *Wessex in the Early Middle Ages* (London: Leicester University Press, 1995)

Glossary

ætheling A member of an Anglo-Saxon royal house, usually with some claim to the throne.

Anglo-Saxon Chronicle the term used to describe the 'national' sets of annals begun in the 9th century by the order of King Alfred (in some cases re-writing old annals for the period up to the 9th century) and which recorded, with varying degrees of truthfulness, events in the Anglo-Saxon kingdoms usually from a West Saxon viewpoint.

burh Old English term for a fortification, or any demarcated place (i.e. with a boundary); since the academic 'discovery' of the value of the *Burghal Hidage*, a document detailing the arrangements for the defence of places, many of which have since become southern English towns, it is often used by historians and archaeologists to describe urban fortifications, although these were not the only forms of burhs in Anglo-Saxon England.

Danelaw the term given to the area under Danish control given by treaty after the defeat of Guthrum by Alfred the Great in 878. The term 'Danelaw' was not a contemporary one, nor did the division remain fixed for long, but distinctions were made between areas under English (or West Saxon/Mercian) and Danish law.

ealdorman Regional official, up to the 9th century in control of areas equating to a shire, but by the 10th century in charge of larger regions (sometimes called *ealdormanries* or *ealdordoms* by historians) where along with legal responsibilities they were tasked with local defence. Ealdormen were replaced by Earls, new men with similar powers, but greater loyalty to the king, following the accession of Cnut the Great in 1016.

fyrd Old English term for an army, usually meaning an expedition. The term is generally used to refer to an army in defence, as opposed to a *Here*, which meant a raiding army, and did not necessarily consist of large numbers of conscripted peasants.

palisade Non-contemporary term used to refer to the wooden structure on top of *ramparts*.

rampart Non-contemporary term used to refer to the collected earthworks that formed early fortifications.

shire From the Old English *scire* meaning 'share', this was a term for the division of the kingdom into administrative areas of England, which became the English counties after the Norman conquest, such as Hampshire, Wiltshire and Worcestershire.

thegn From an Old English term meaning 'servant', this came to mean a warrior of status with obligations to fight for the king.

Index

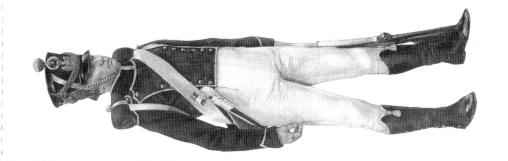

FIND OUT MORE ABOUT OSPREY

❑ Please send me the latest listing of Osprey's publications

❑ I would like to subscribe to Osprey's e-mail newsletter

Title / rank

Name

Address

City / county

Postcode / zip   state / country

e-mail

I am interested in:

❑ Ancient world
❑ Medieval world
❑ 16th century
❑ 17th century
❑ 18th century
❑ Napoleonic
❑ 19th century

❑ American Civil War
❑ World War 1
❑ World War 2
❑ Modern warfare
❑ Military aviation
❑ Naval warfare

Please send to:

USA & Canada:
Osprey Direct USA, c/o MBI Publishing, P.O. Box 1, 729 Prospect Avenue, Osceola, WI 54020

UK, Europe and rest of world:
Osprey Direct UK, P.O. Box 140, Wellingborough, Northants, NN8 2FA, United Kingdom

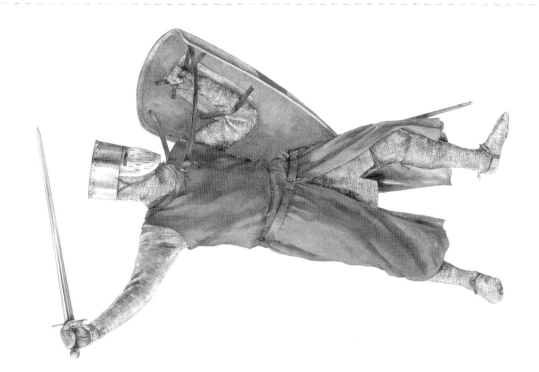

OSPREY
PUBLISHING

www.ospreypublishing.com

call our telephone hotline
for a free information pack

USA & Canada: 1-800-826-6600
UK, Europe and rest of world call:
+44 (0) 1933 443 863

Young Guardsman
Figure taken from Warrior 22:
Imperial Guardsman 1799–1815
Published by Osprey
Illustrated by Christa Hook

Knight, c.1190
Figure taken from *Warrior 1: Norman Knight 950 – 1204 AD*
Published by Osprey
Illustrated by Christa Hook

POSTCARD